Essence of Damian Draco

Essence of Damian Draco

Damian Draco

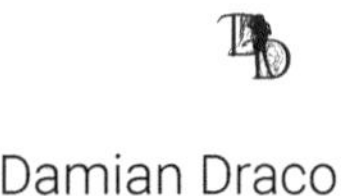

Damian Draco

First Printing, 2024

ISBN: 979-8-3302-6347-9
EISBN: 979-8-3302-6353-0

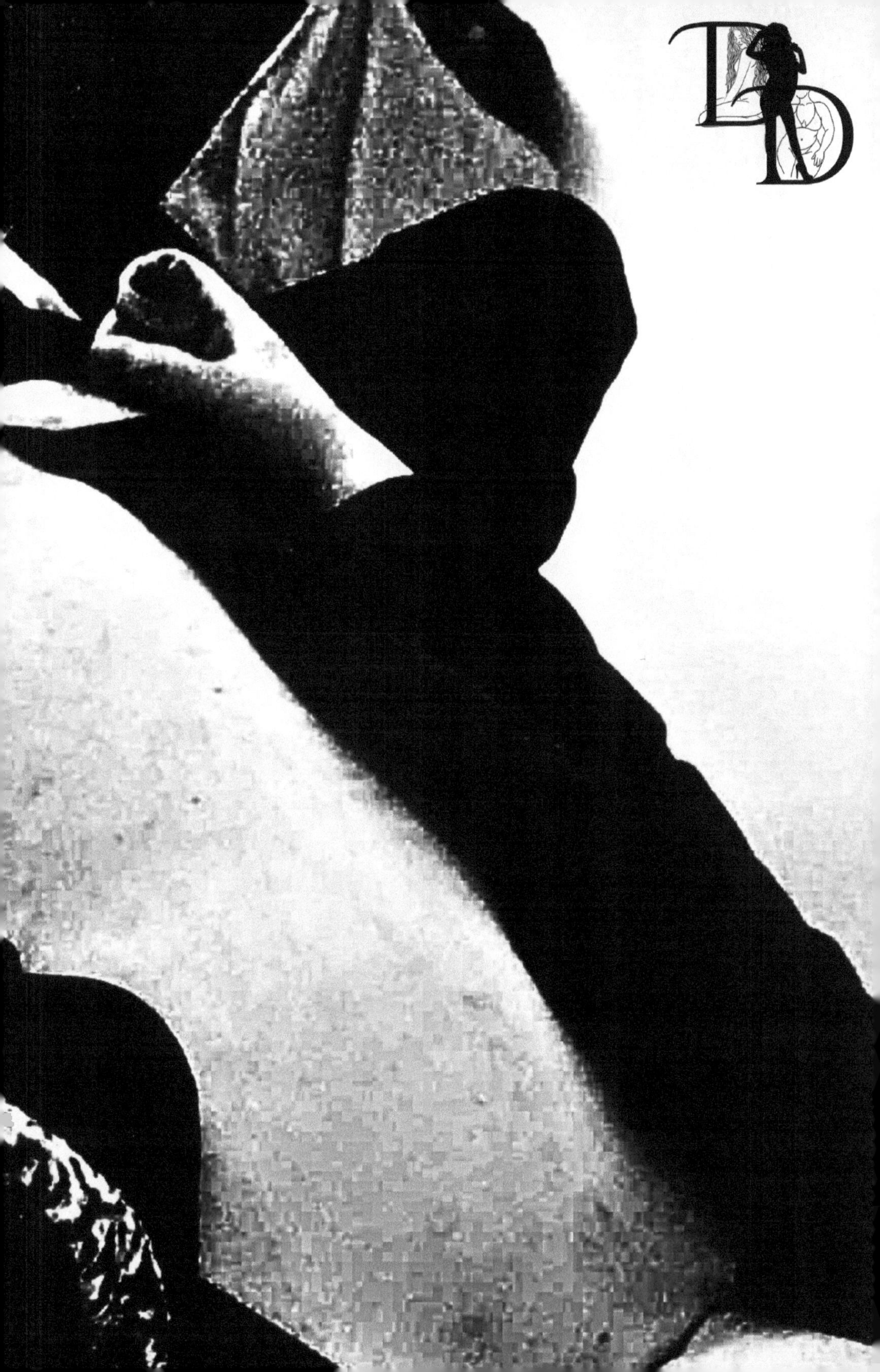

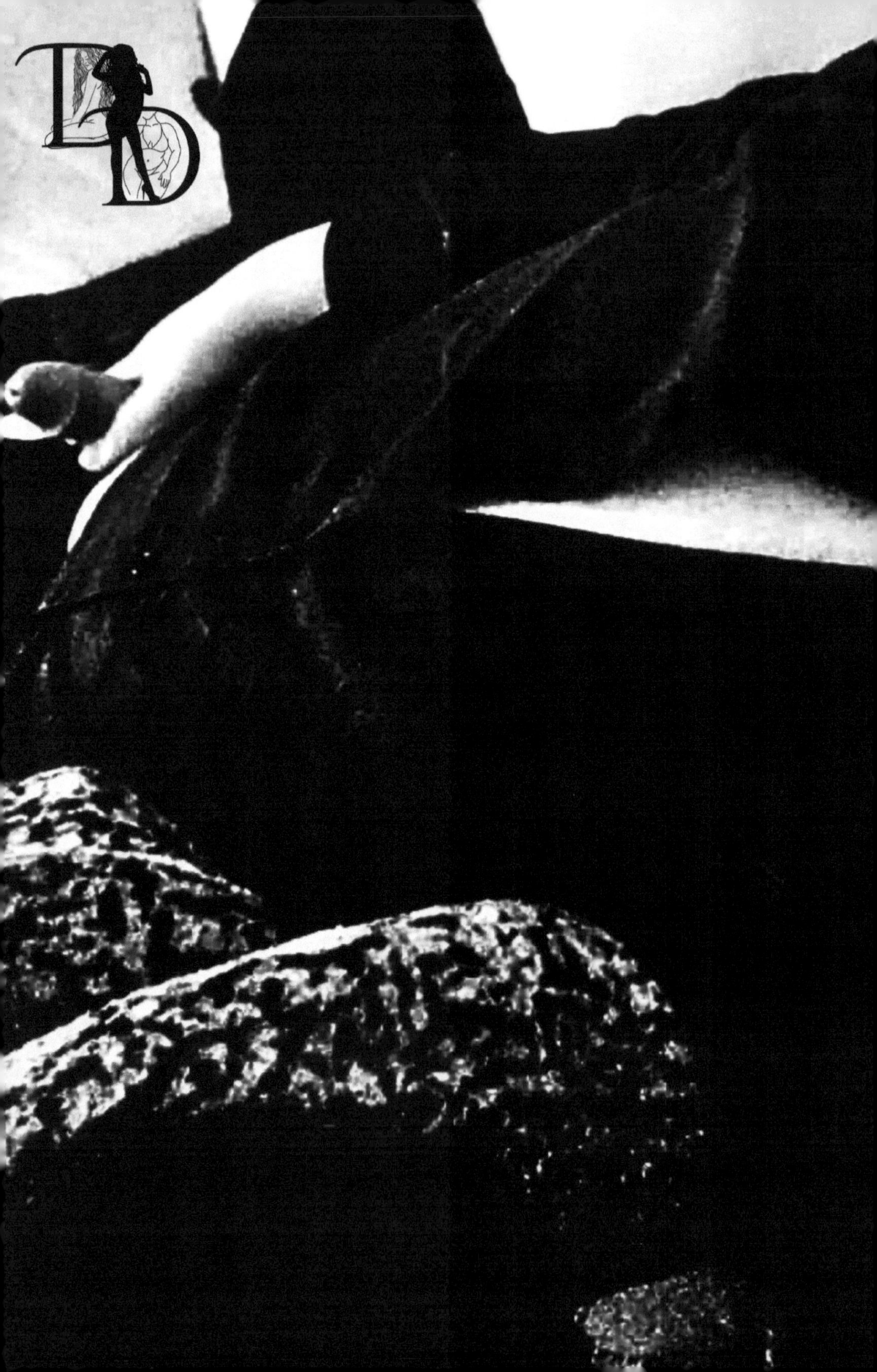

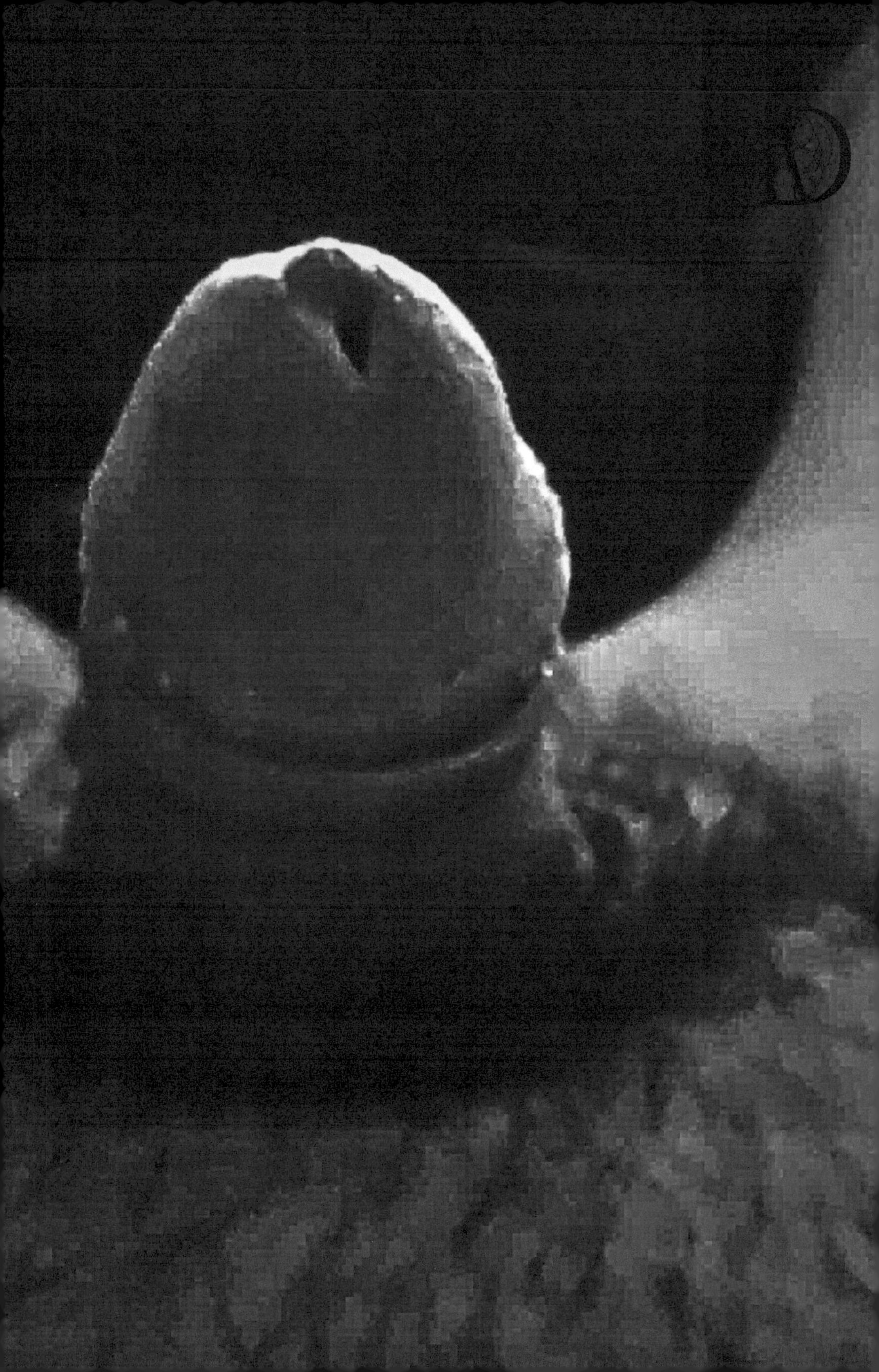

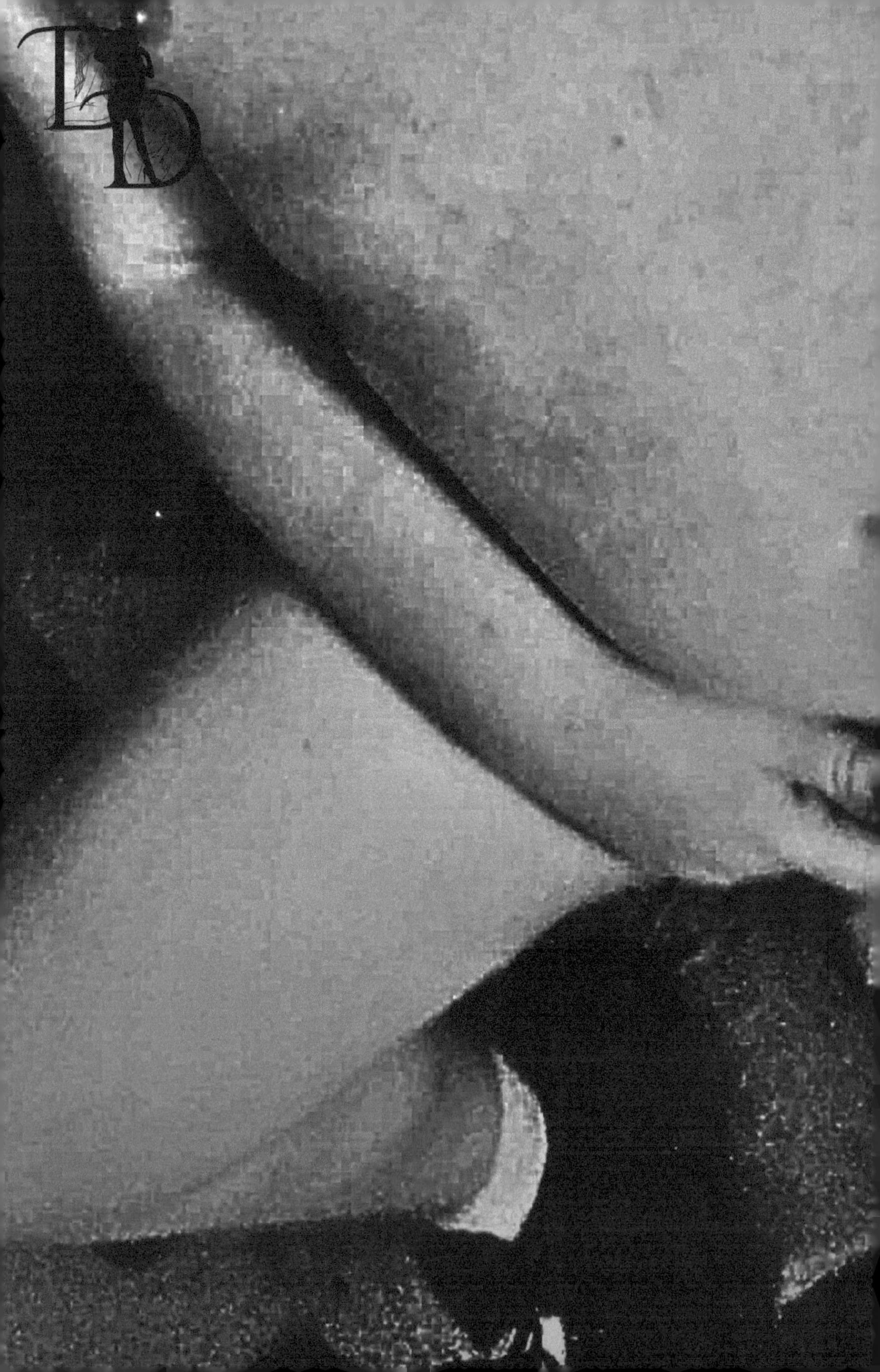

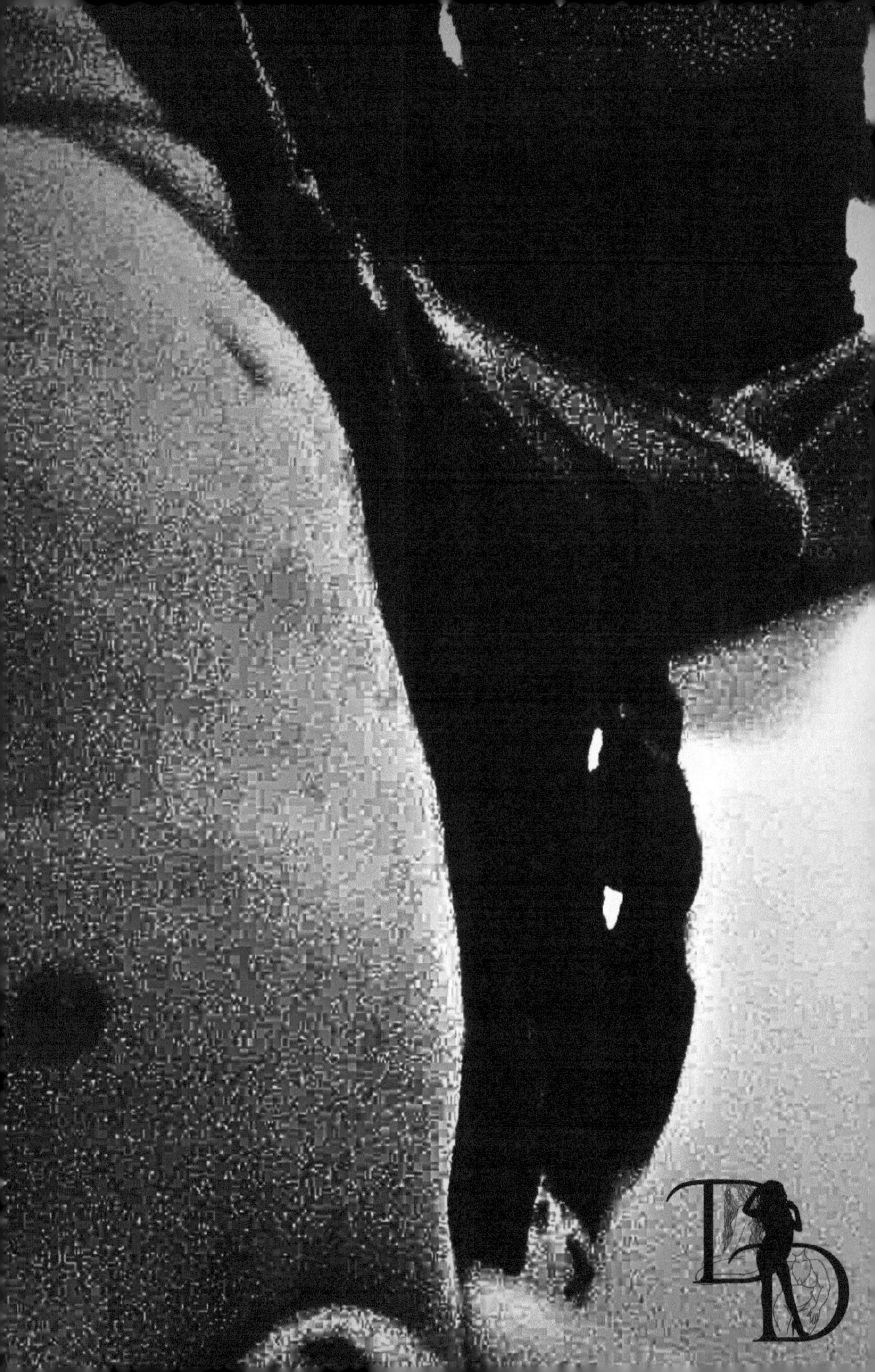

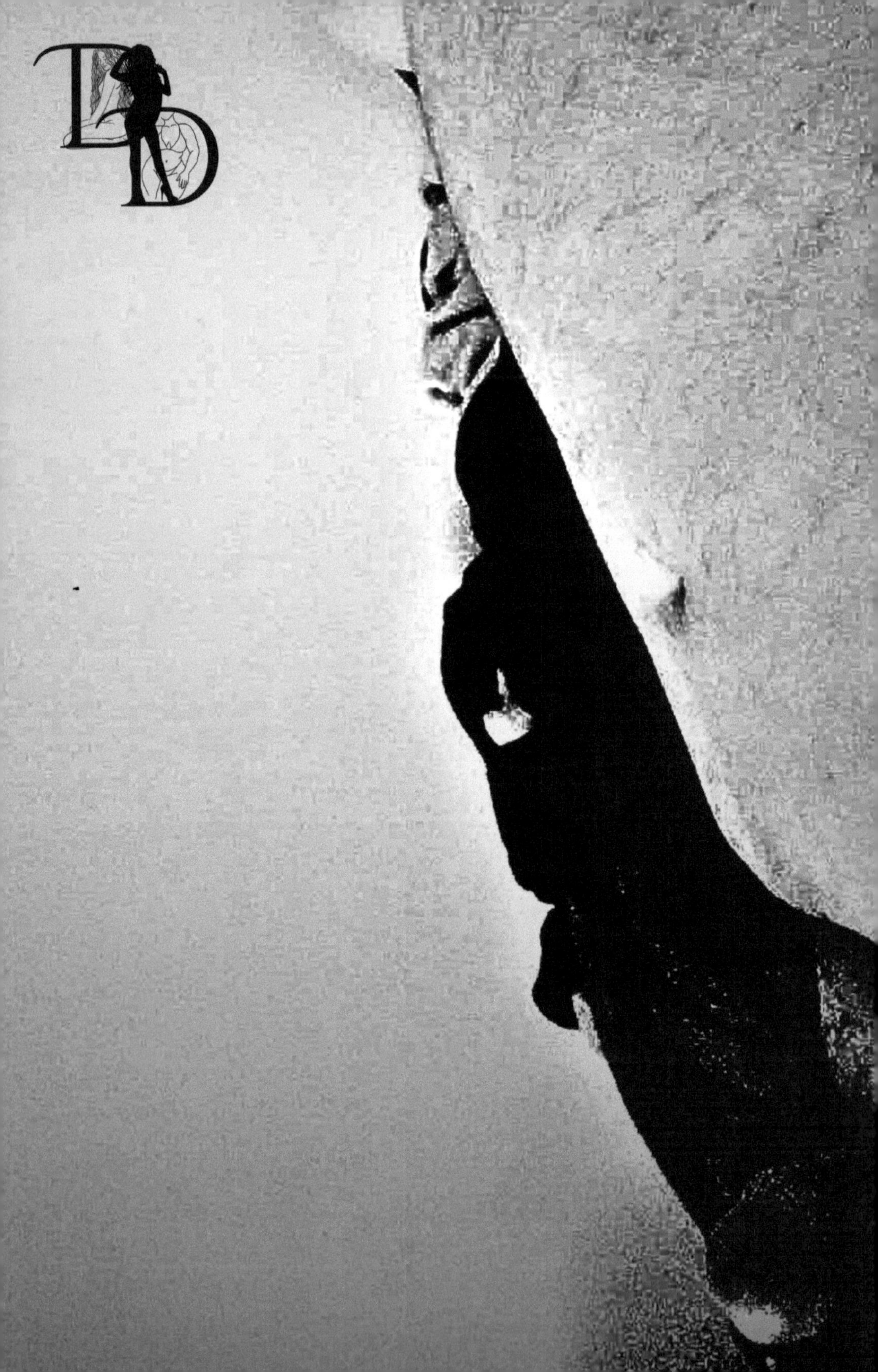

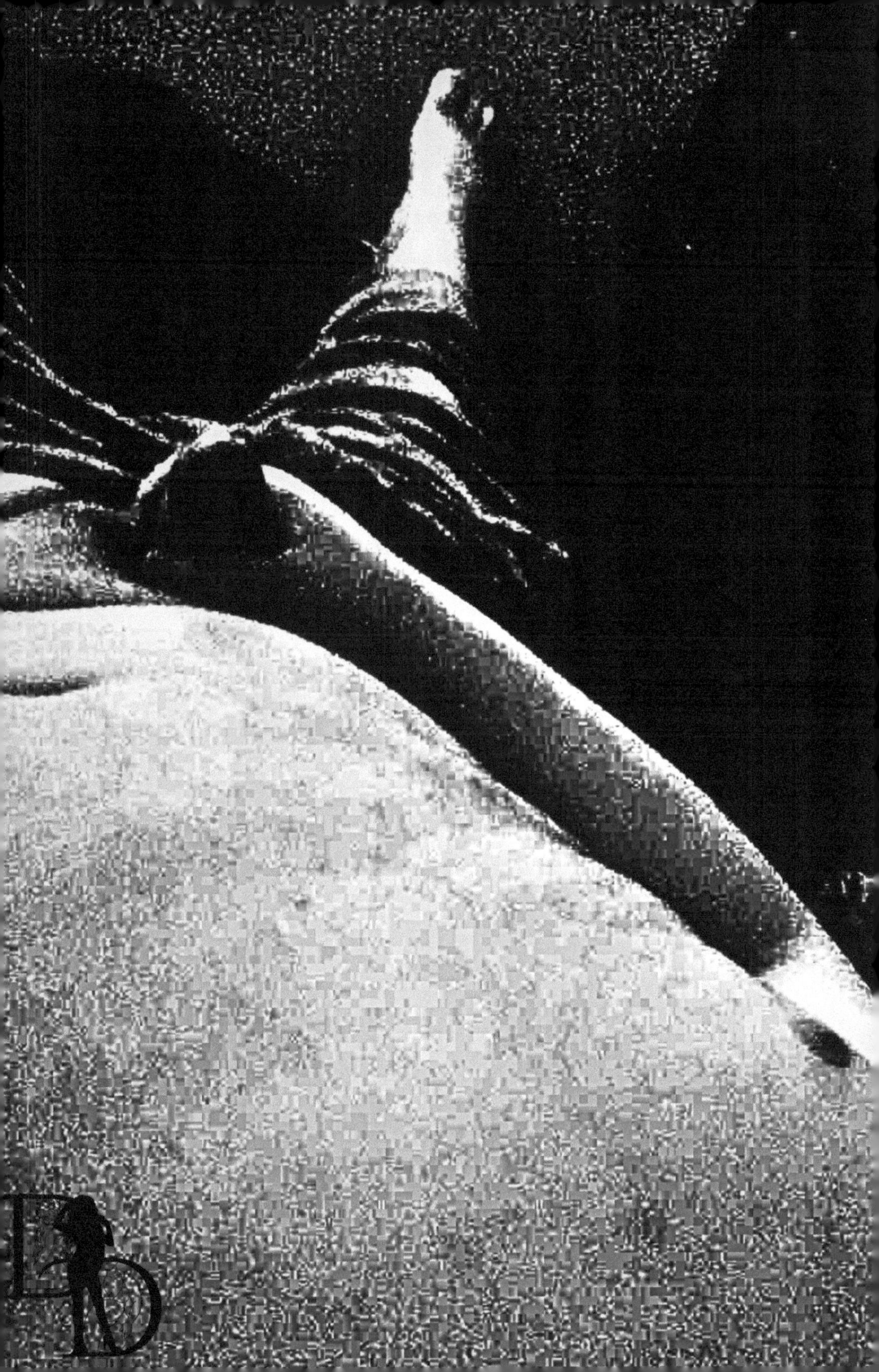

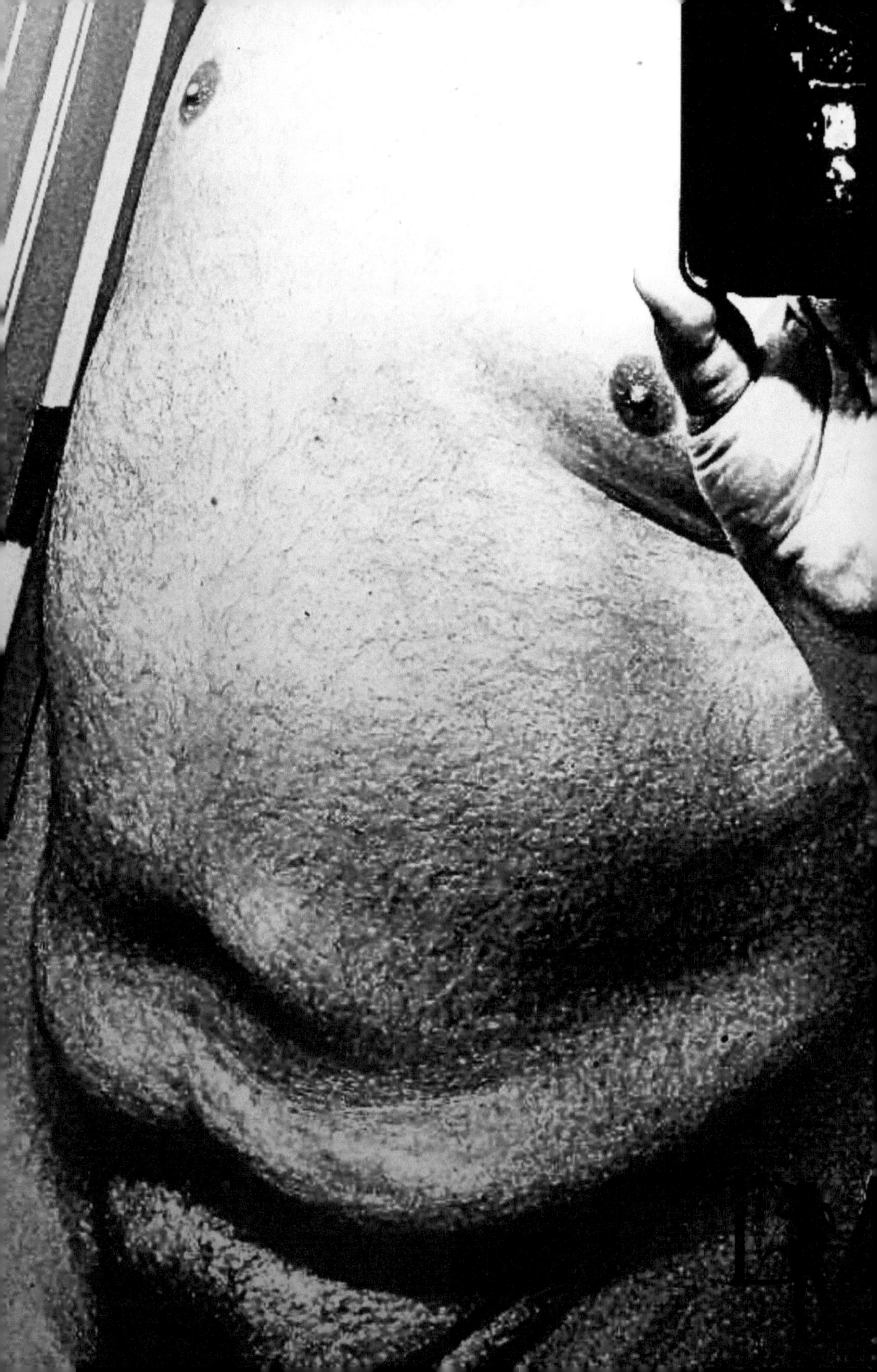

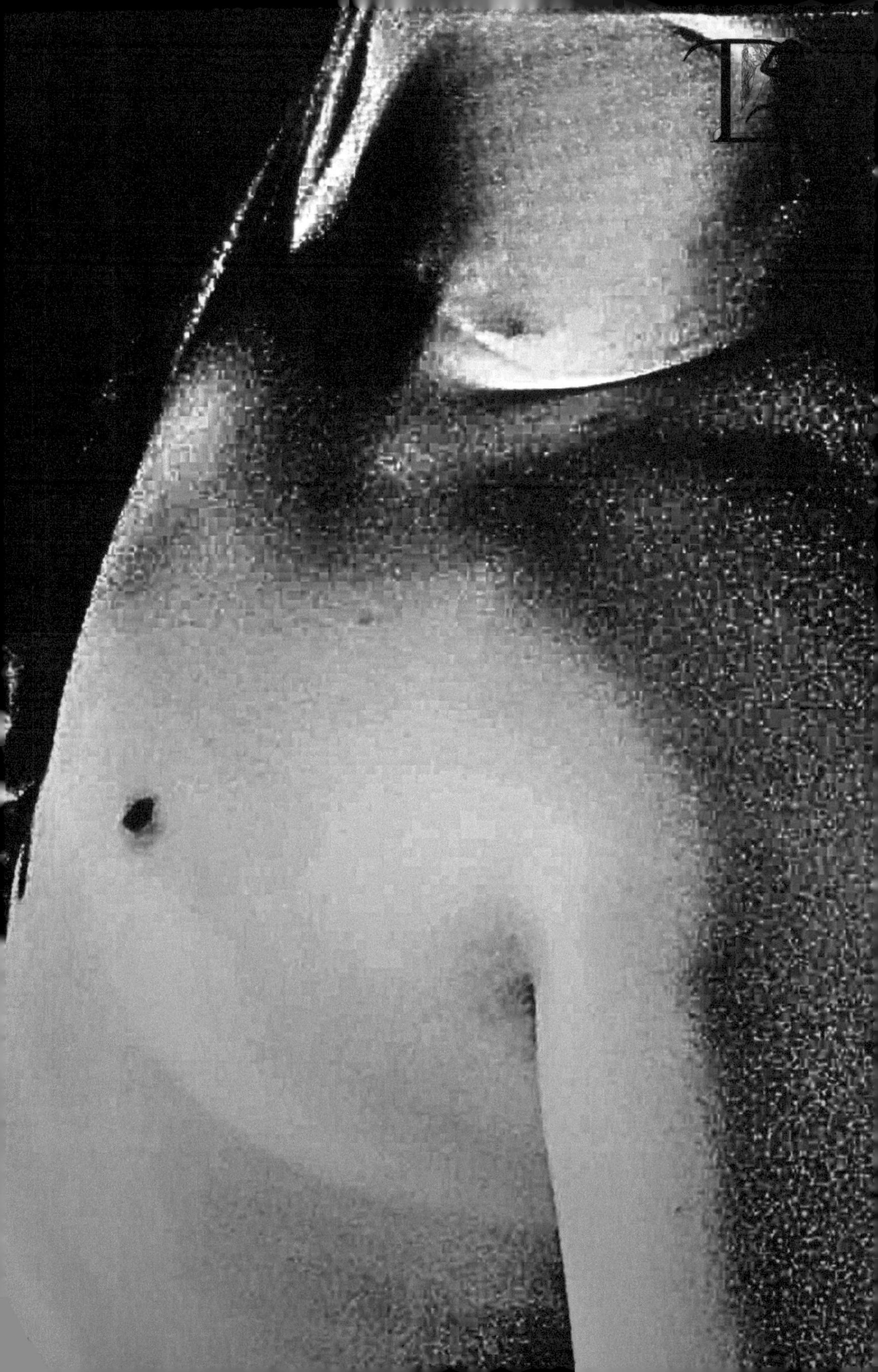

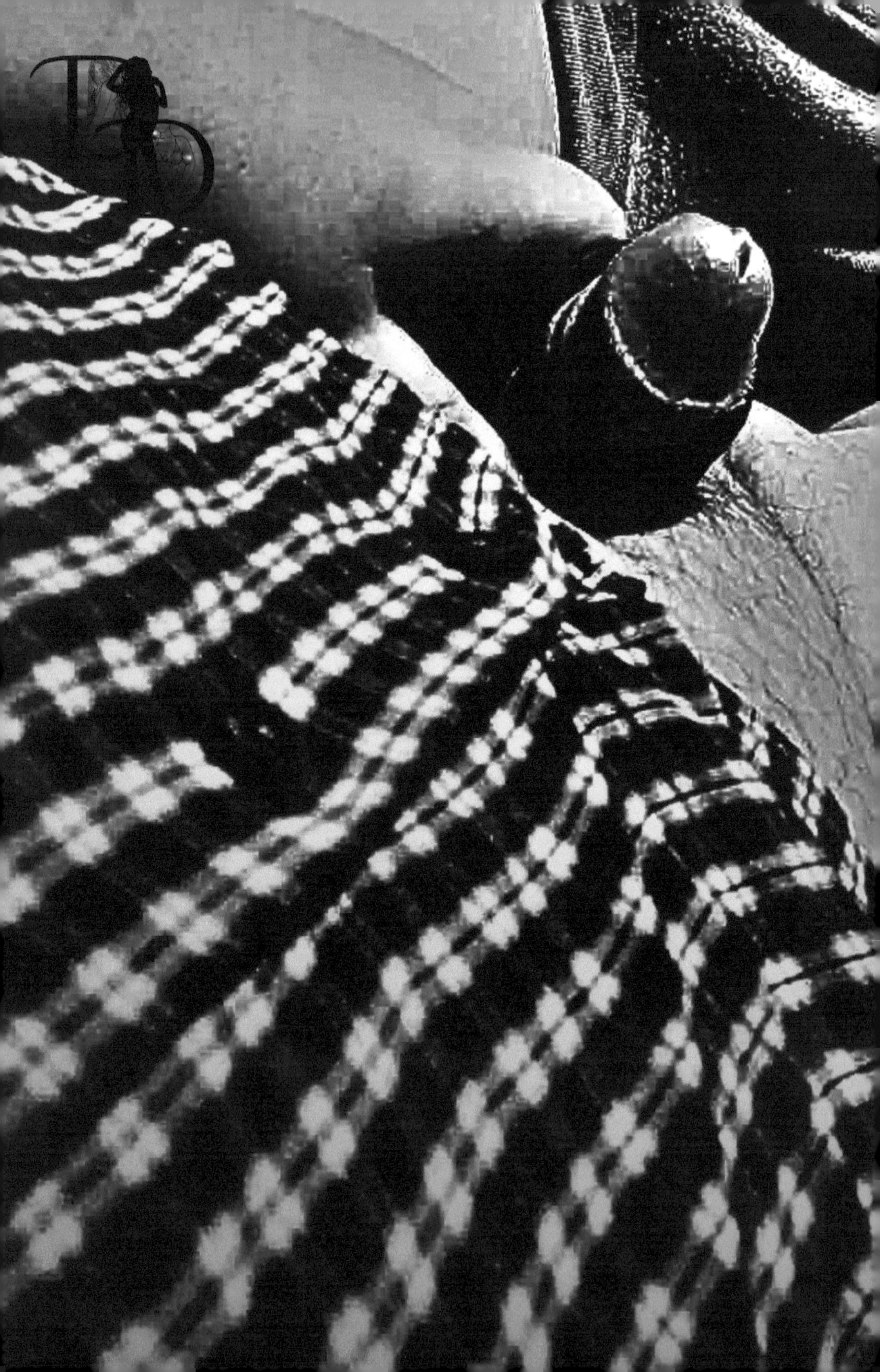

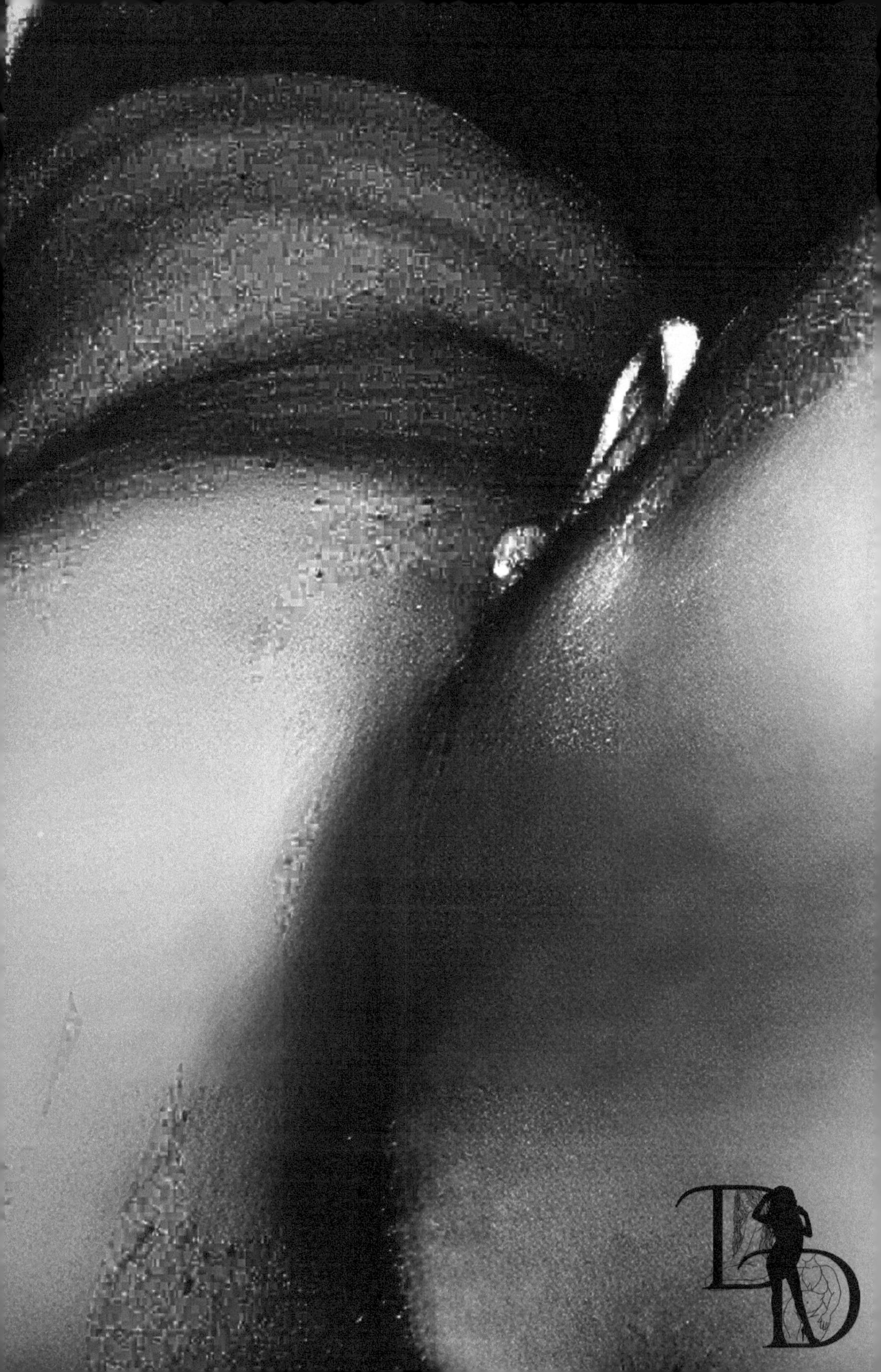

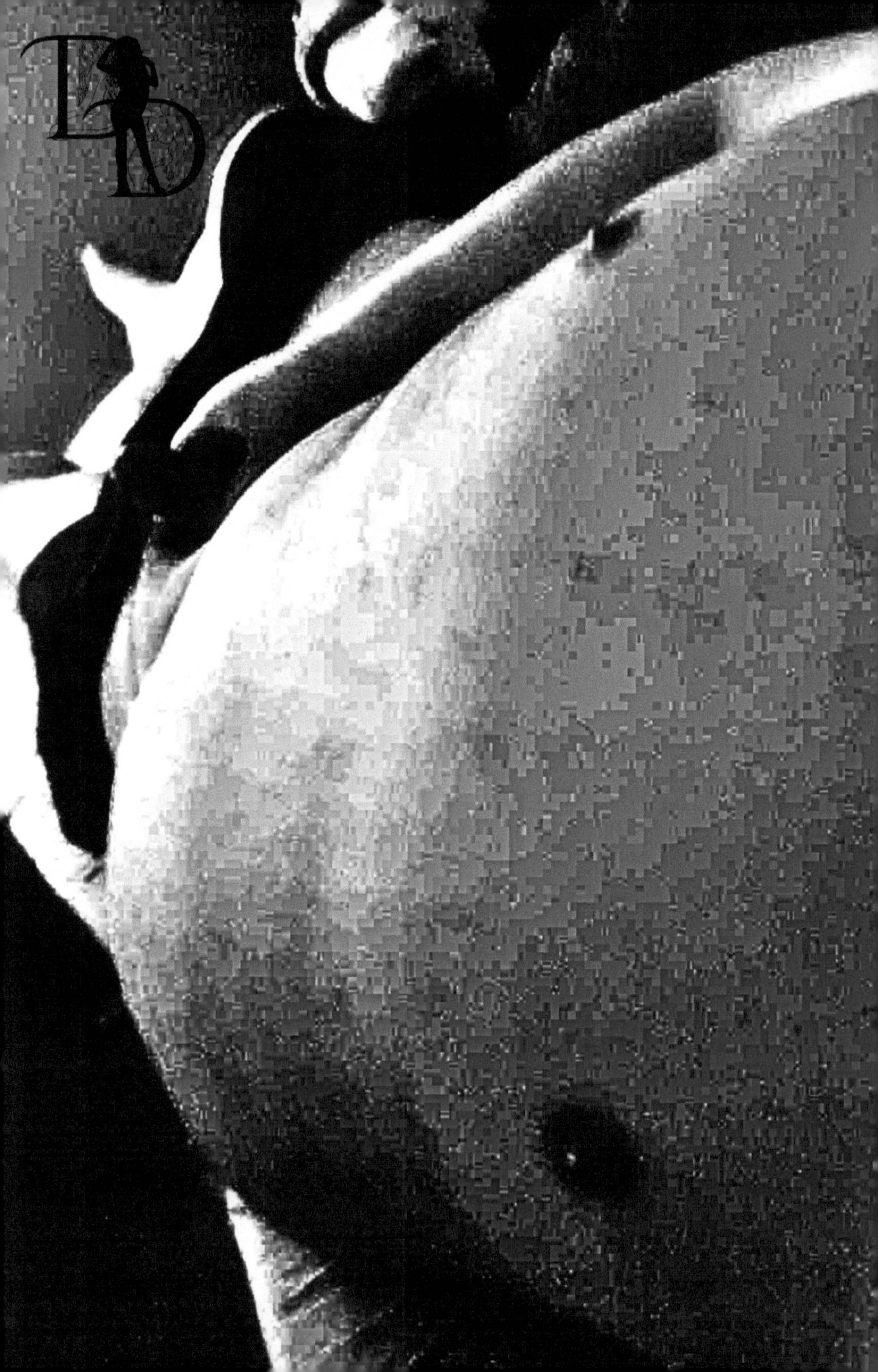

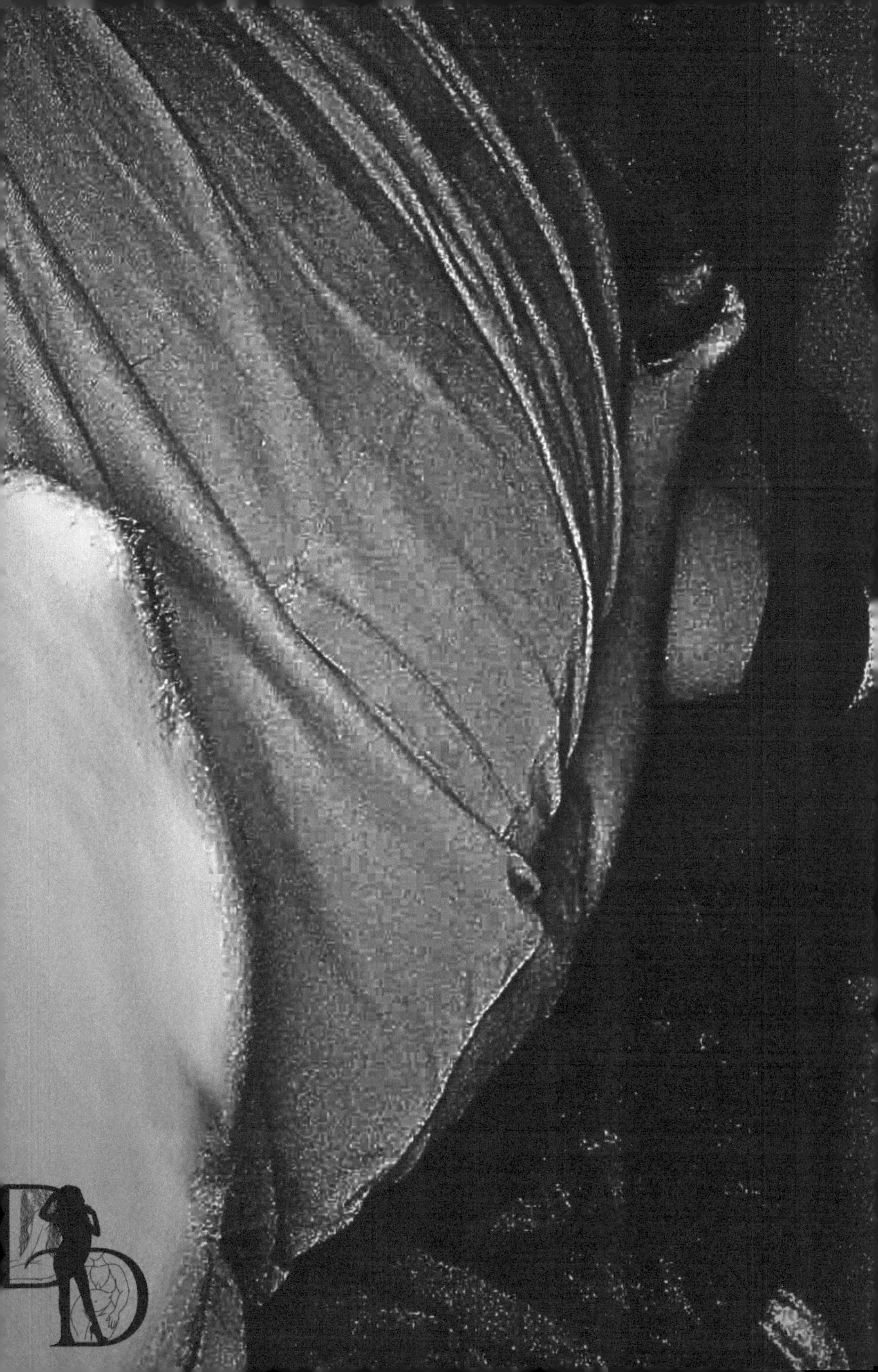

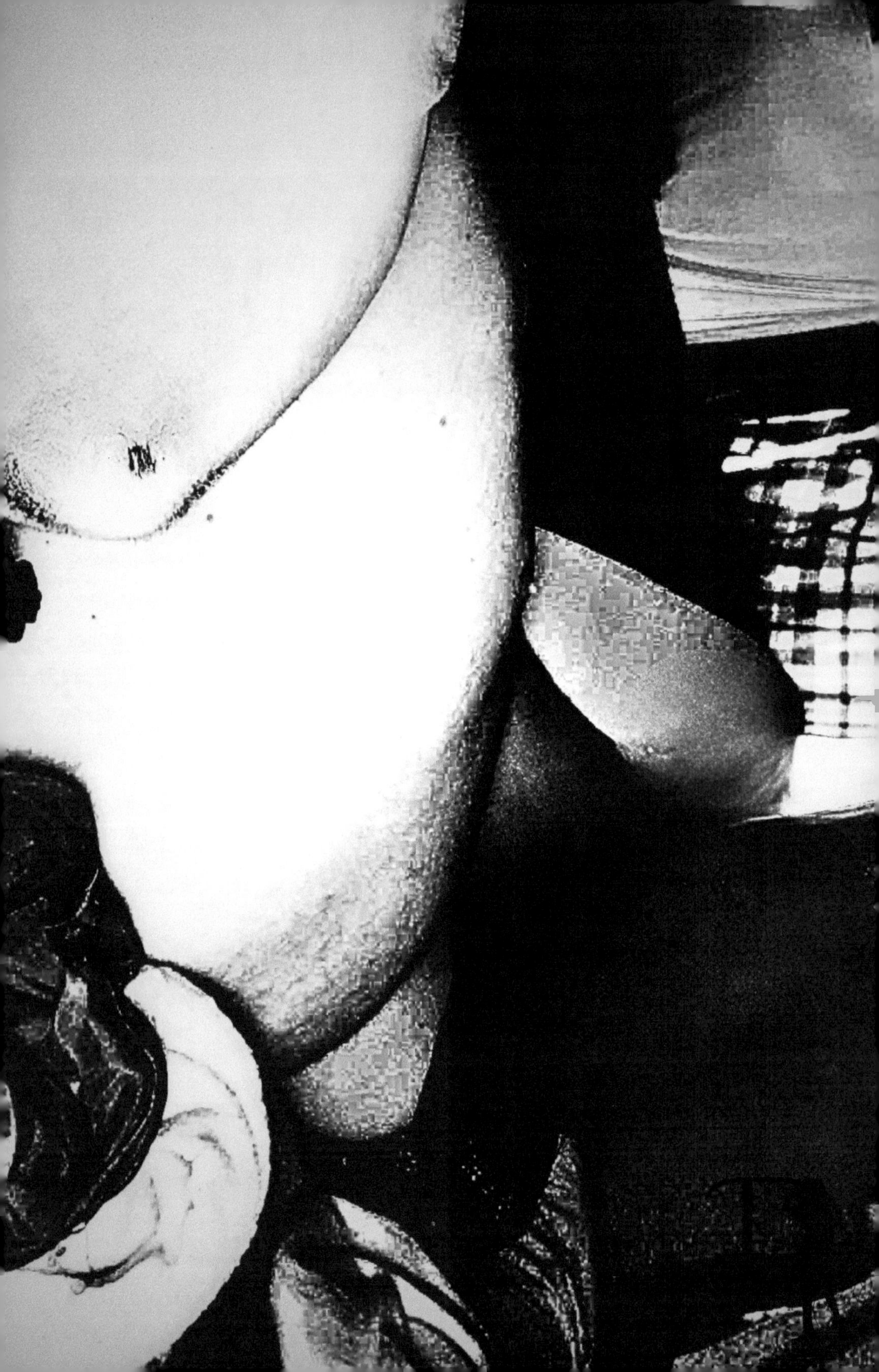

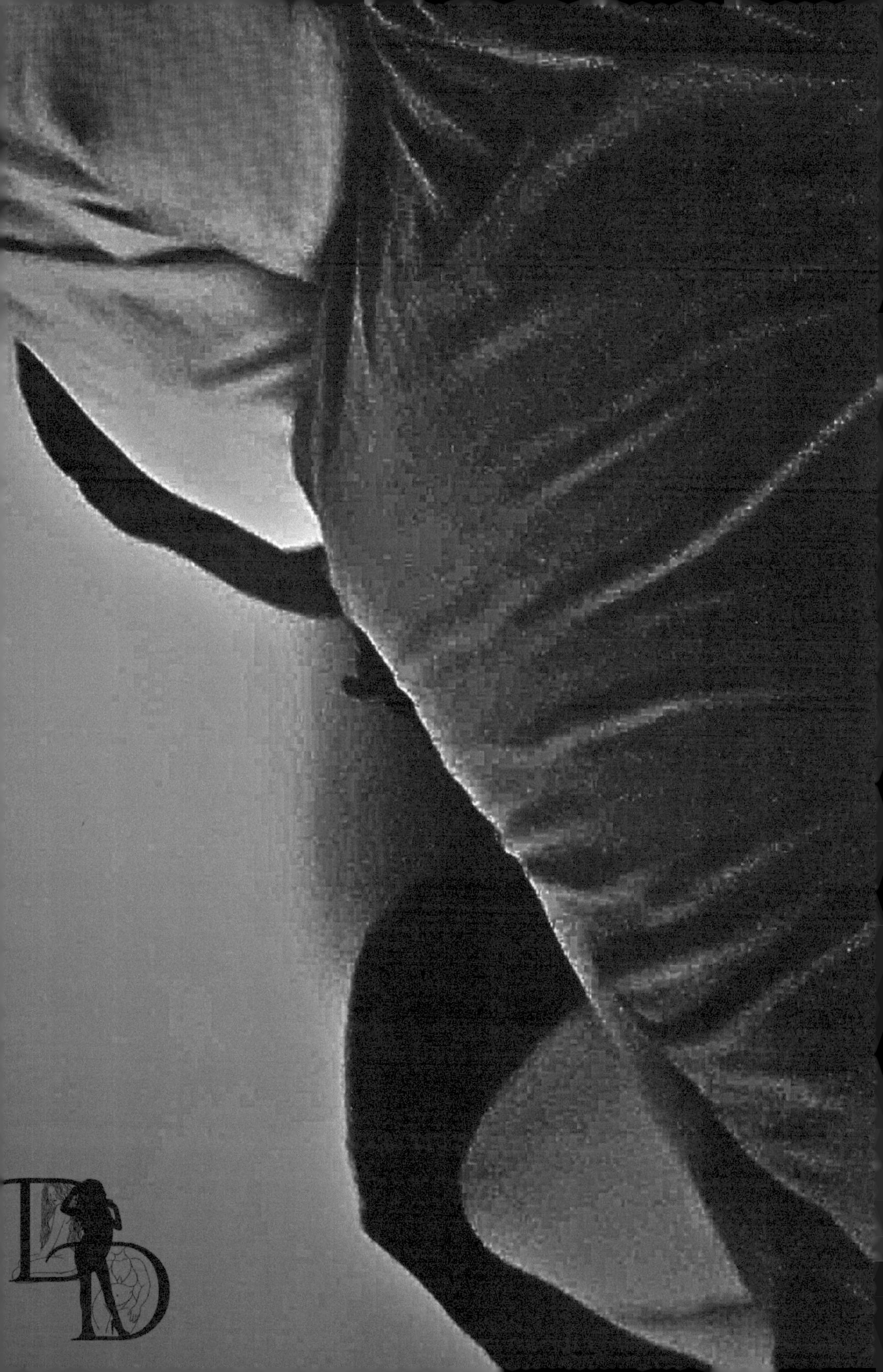

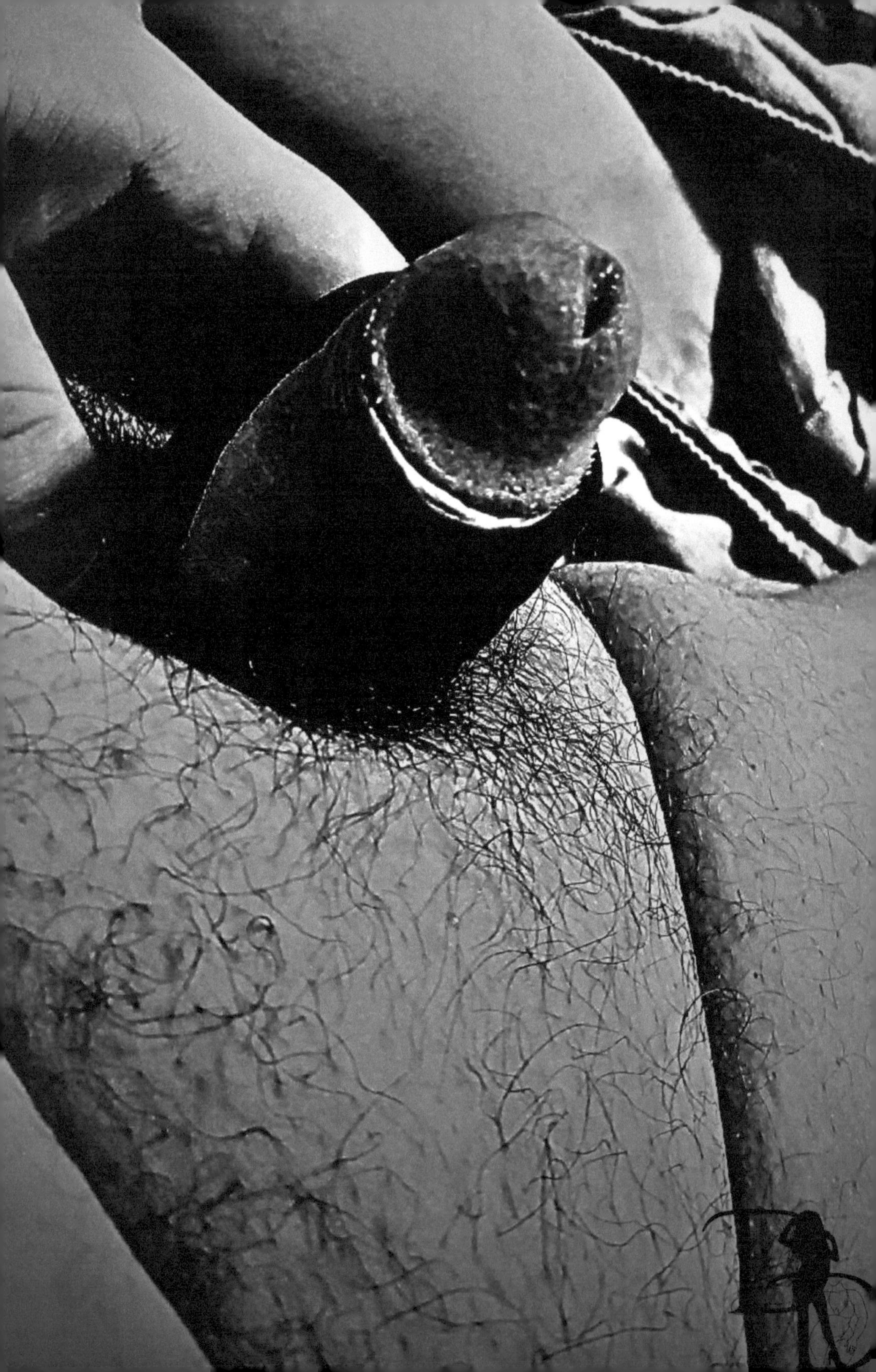

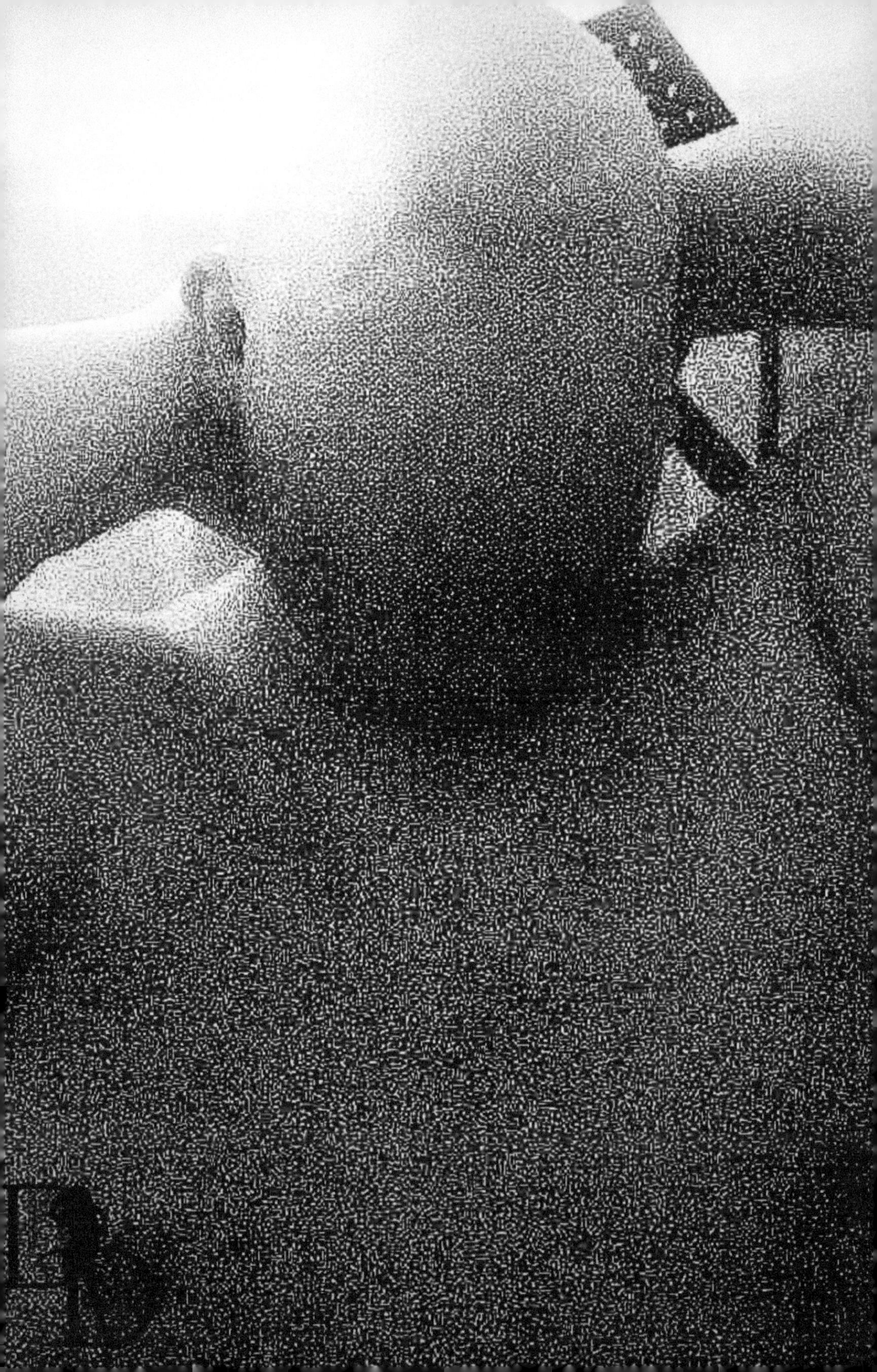

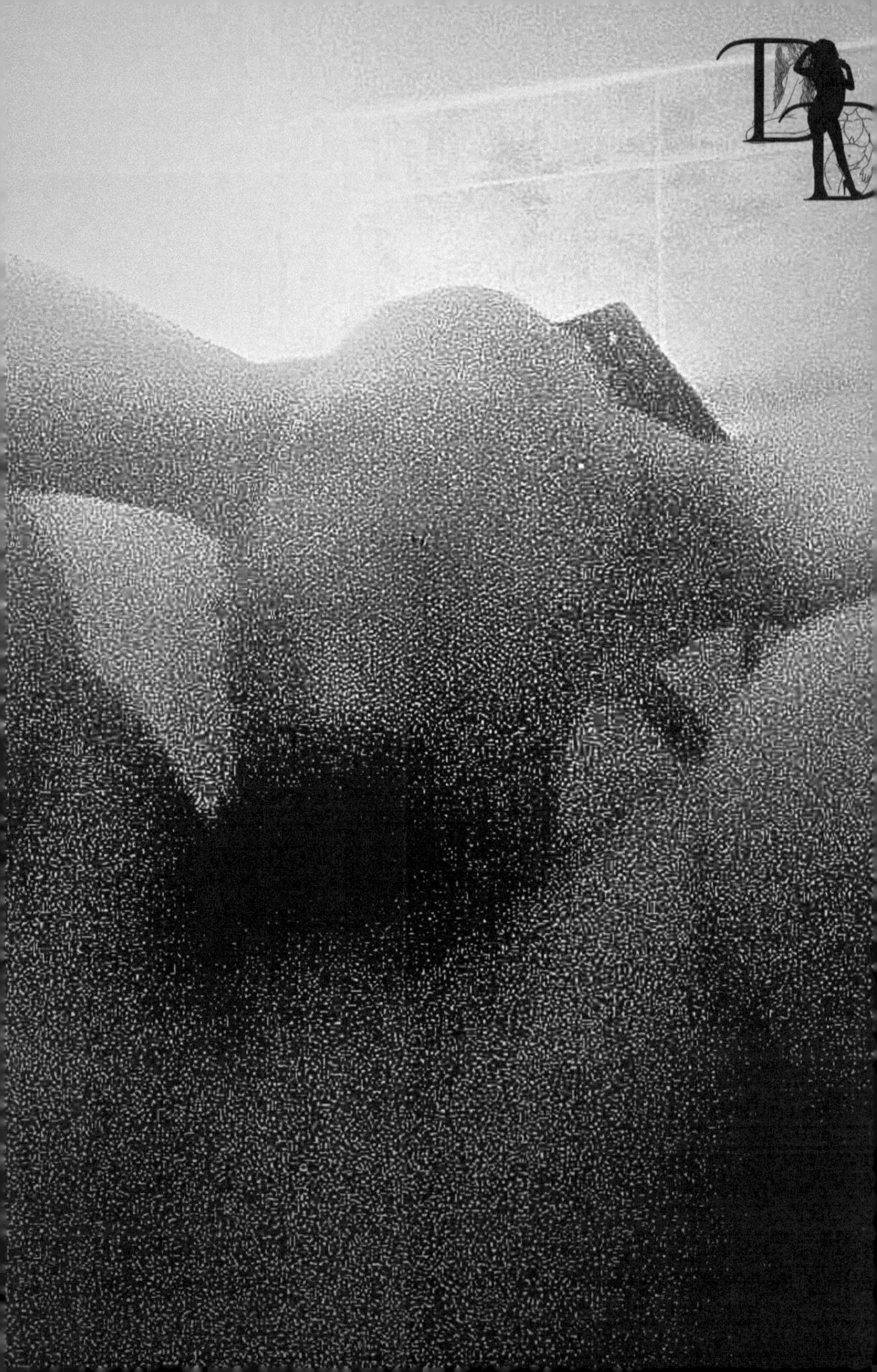

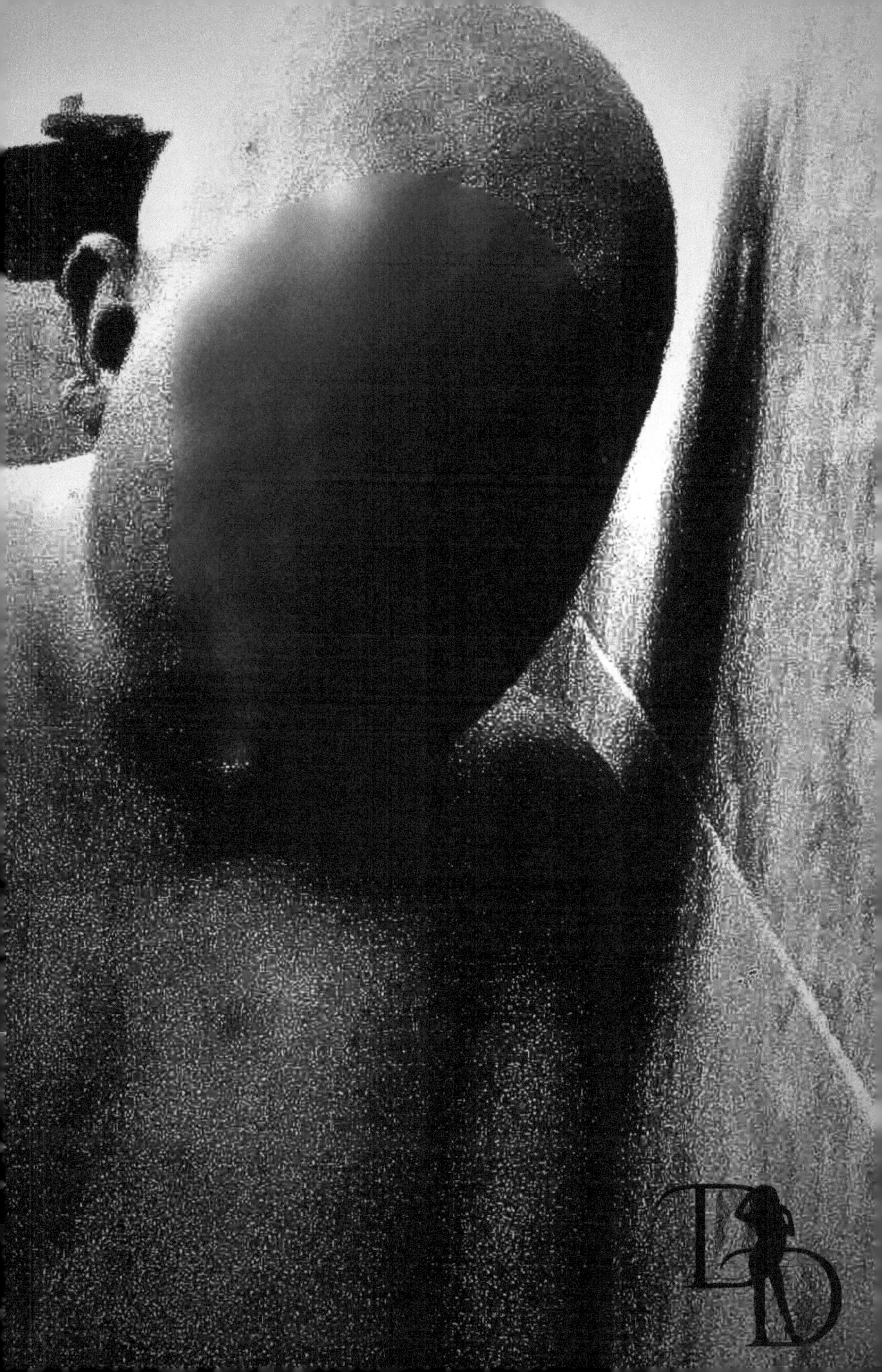

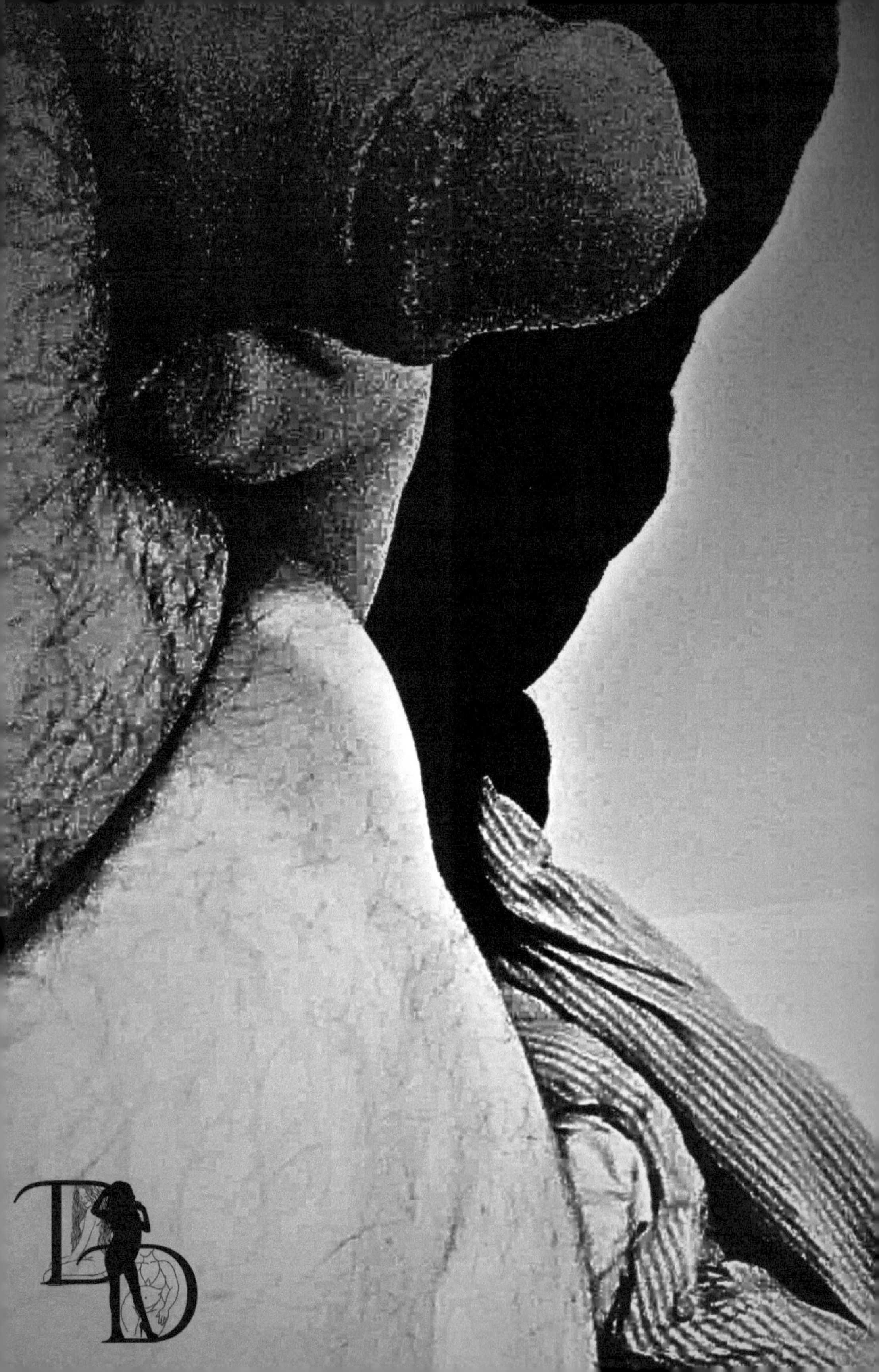

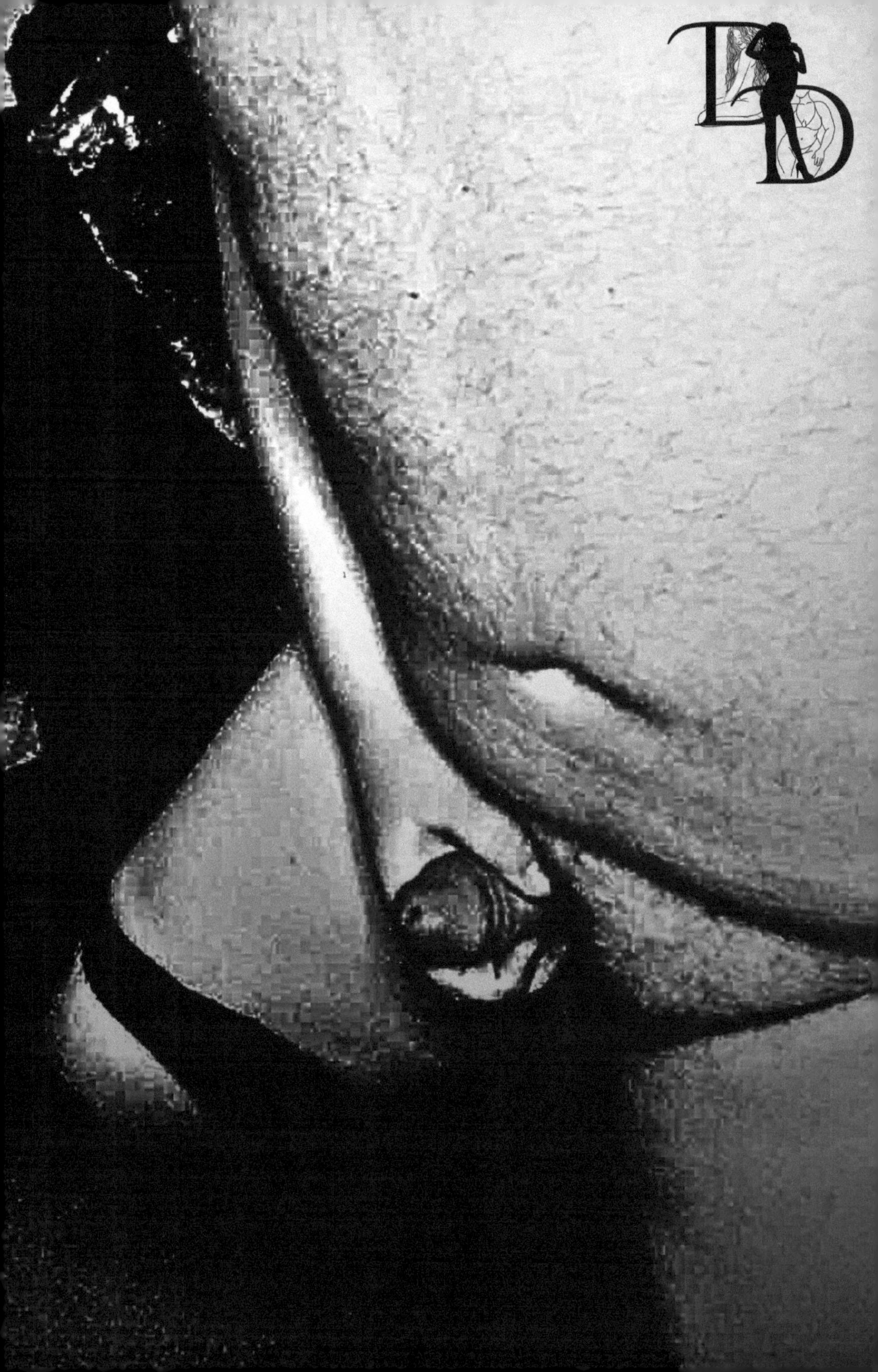

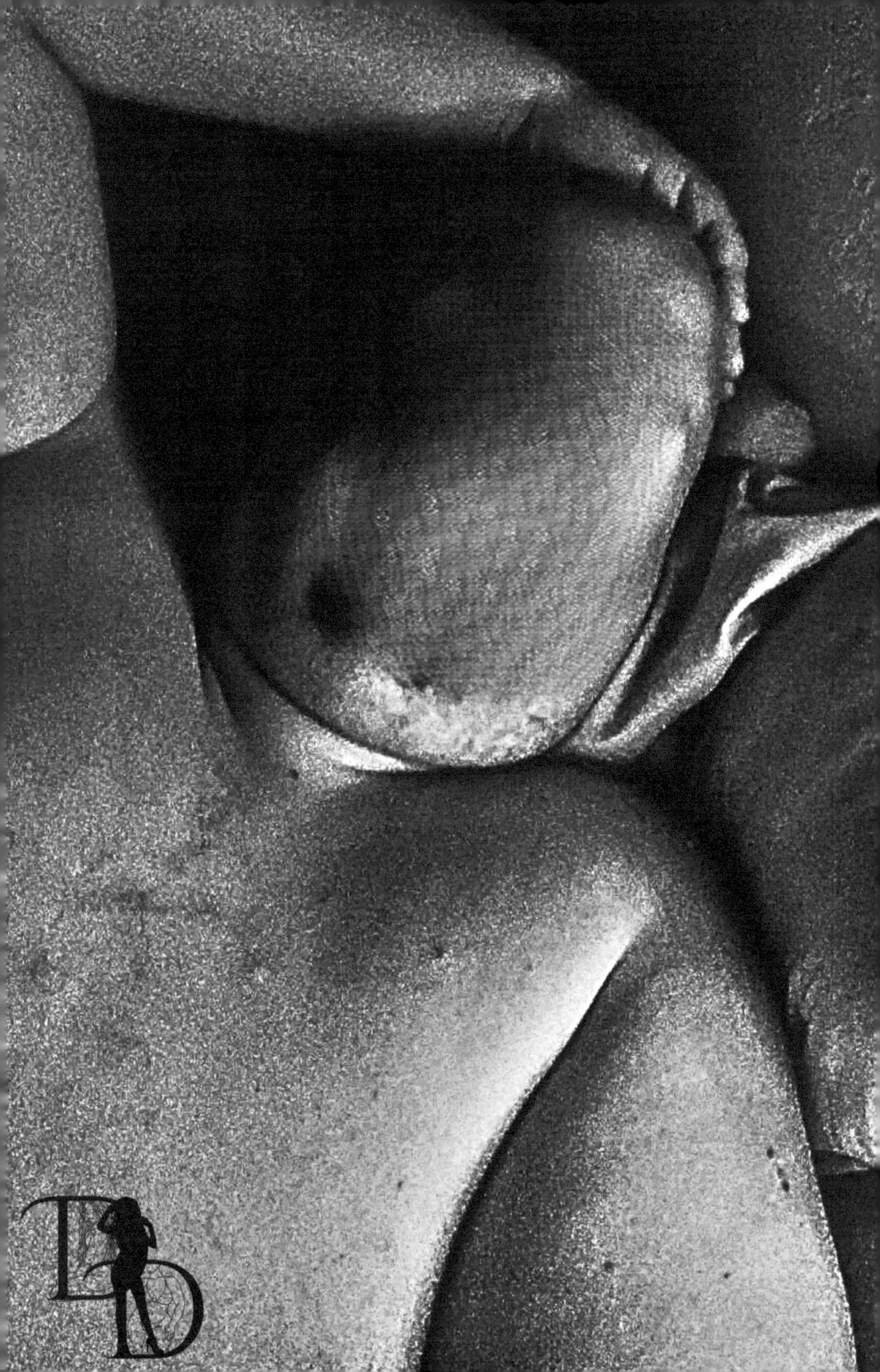

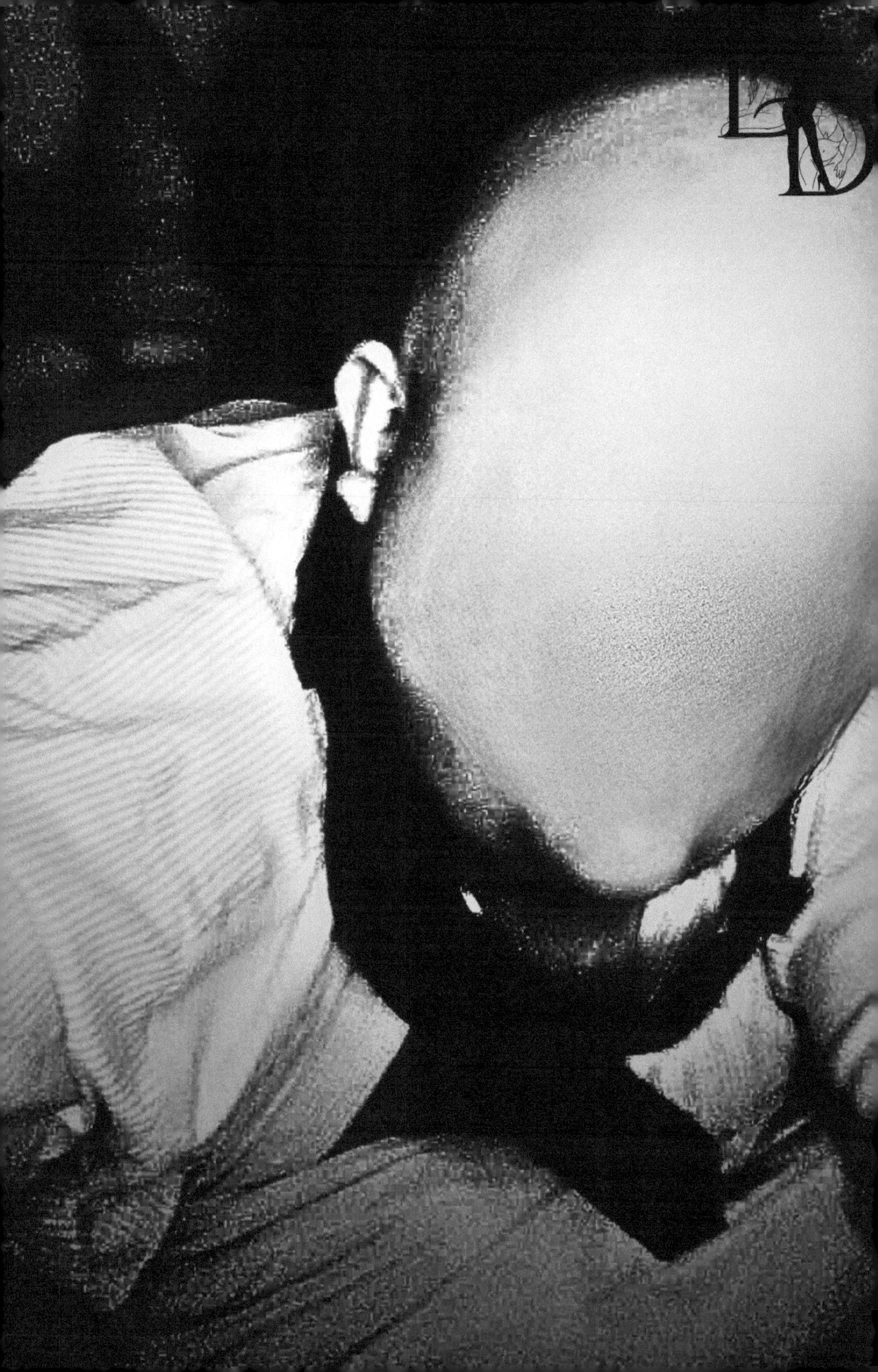

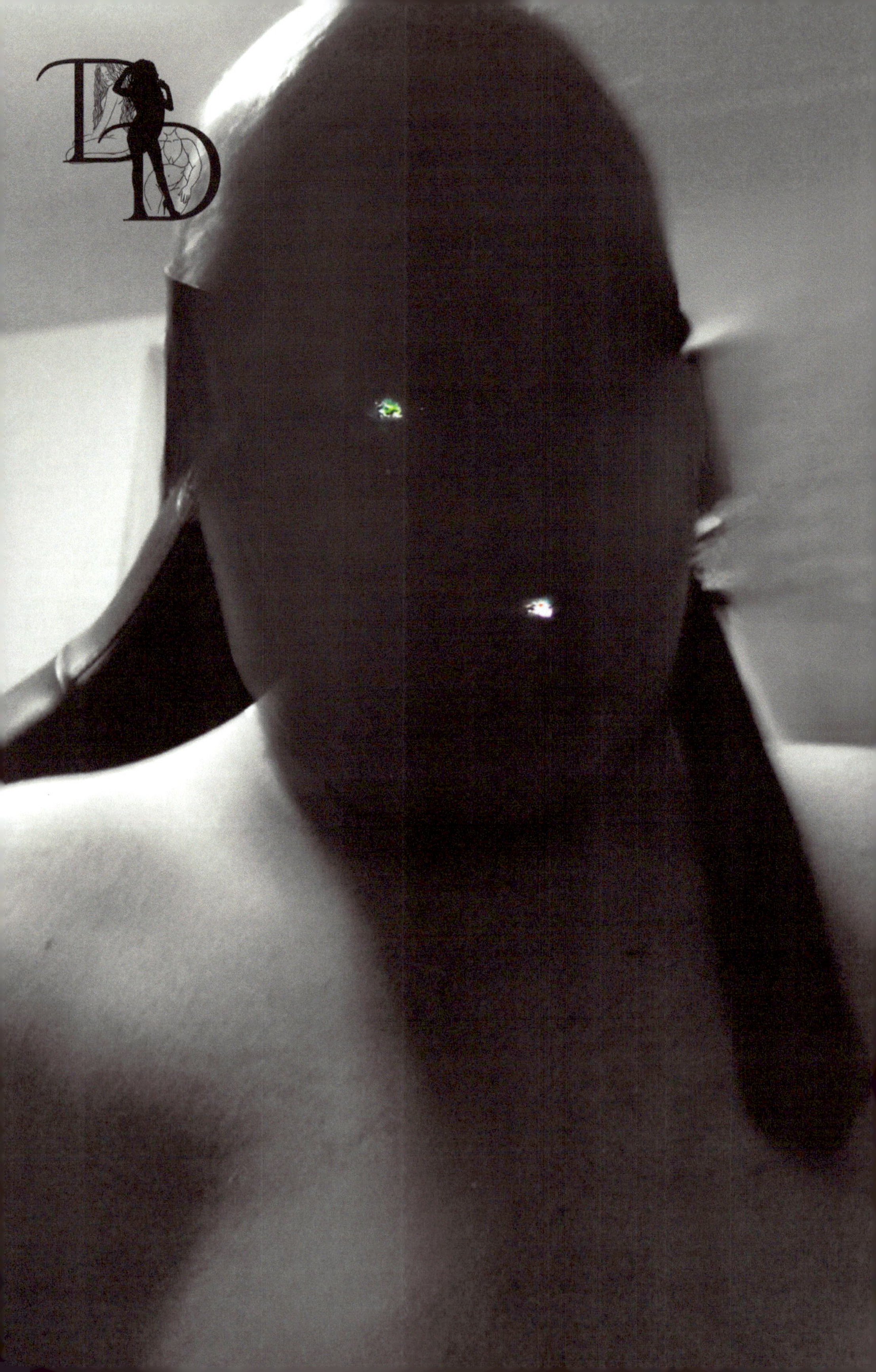

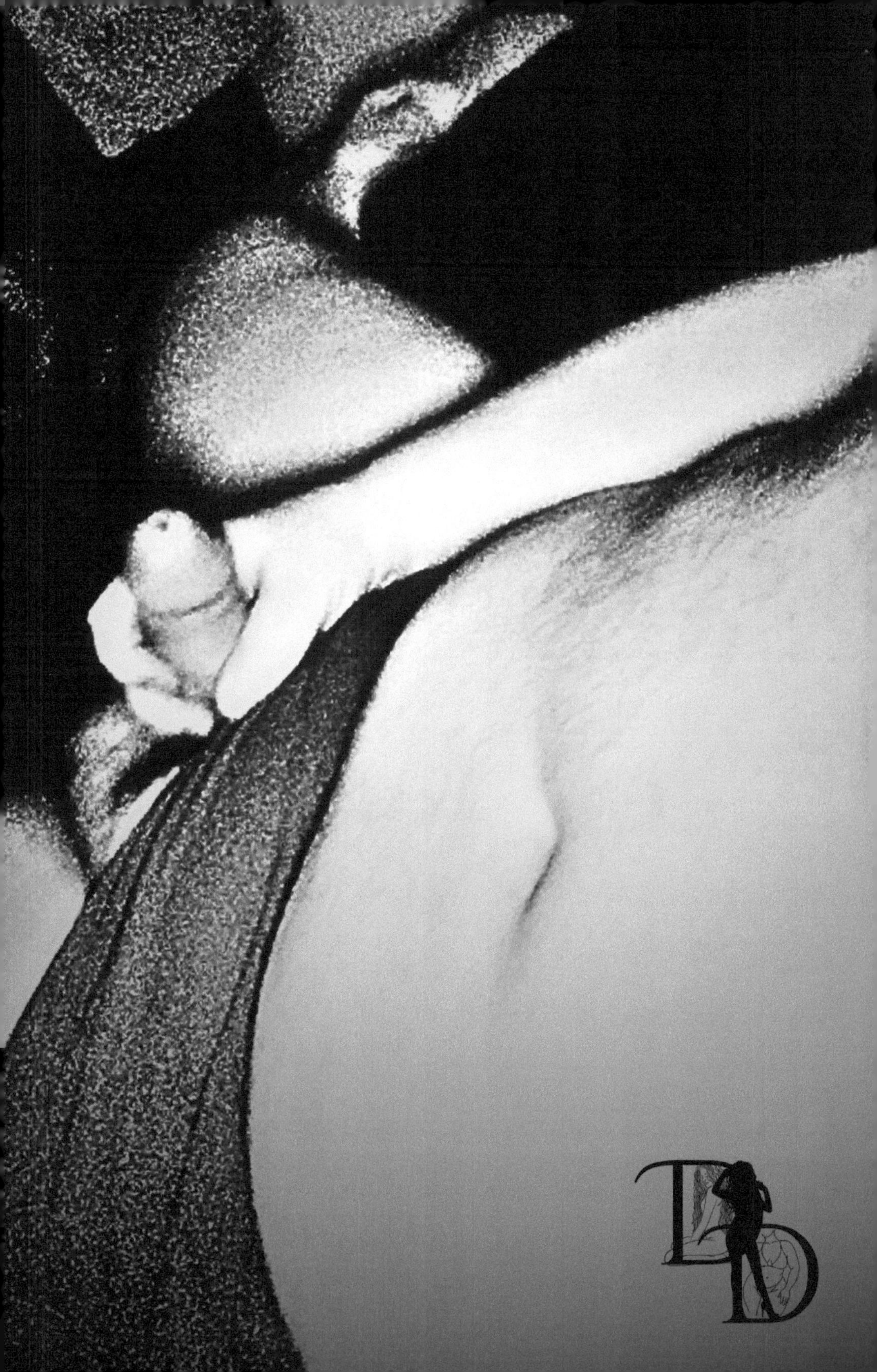

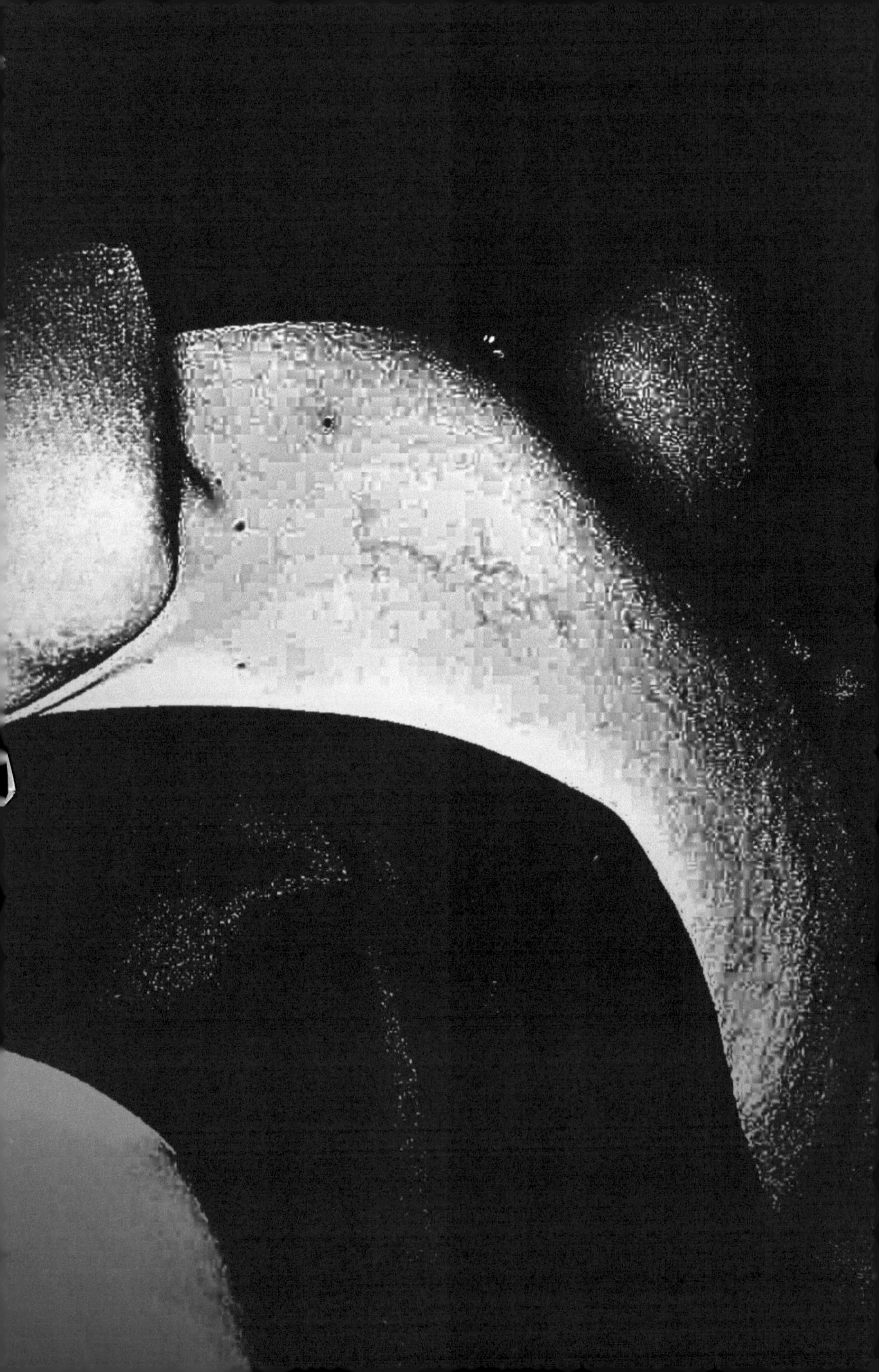

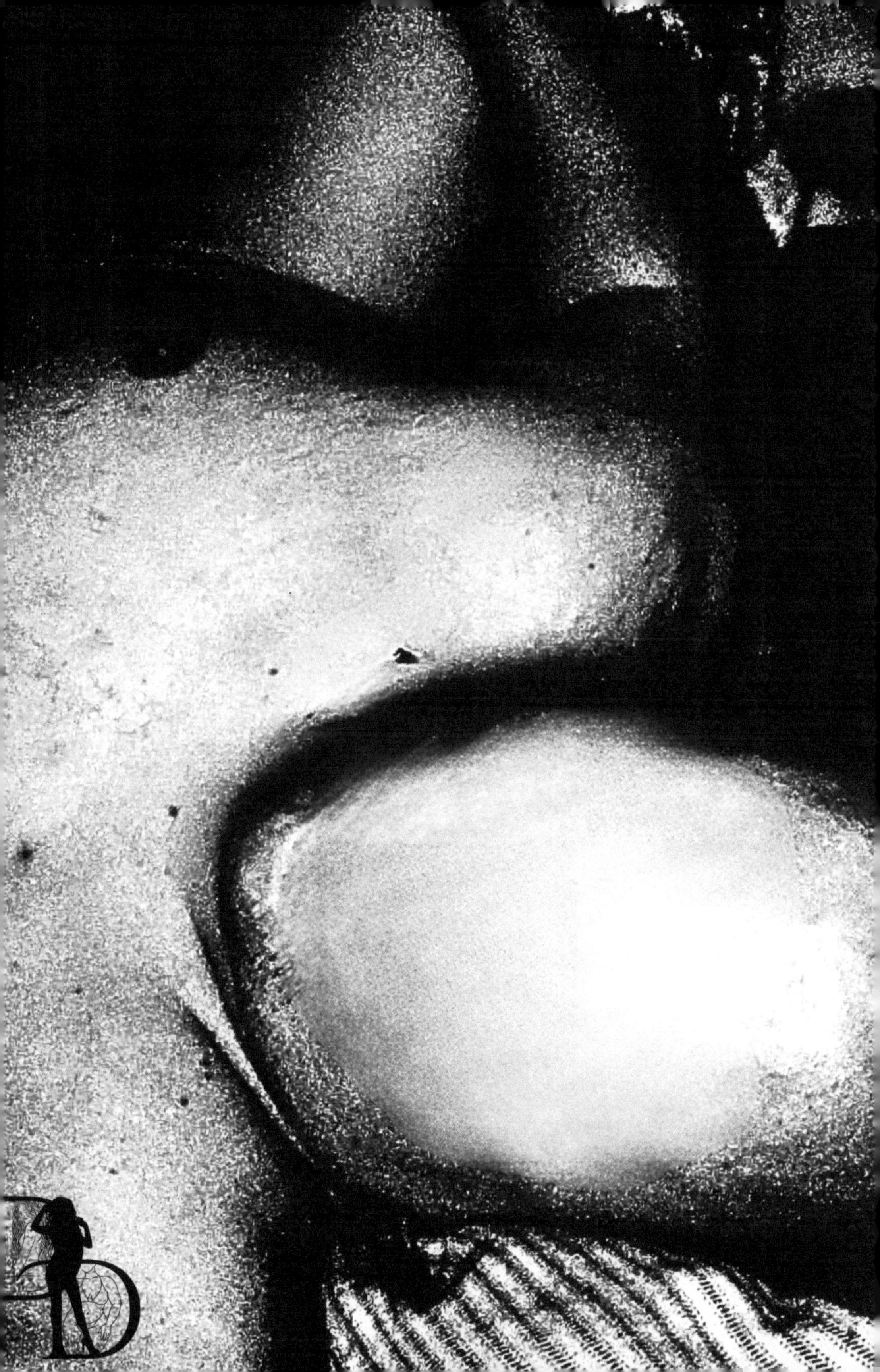

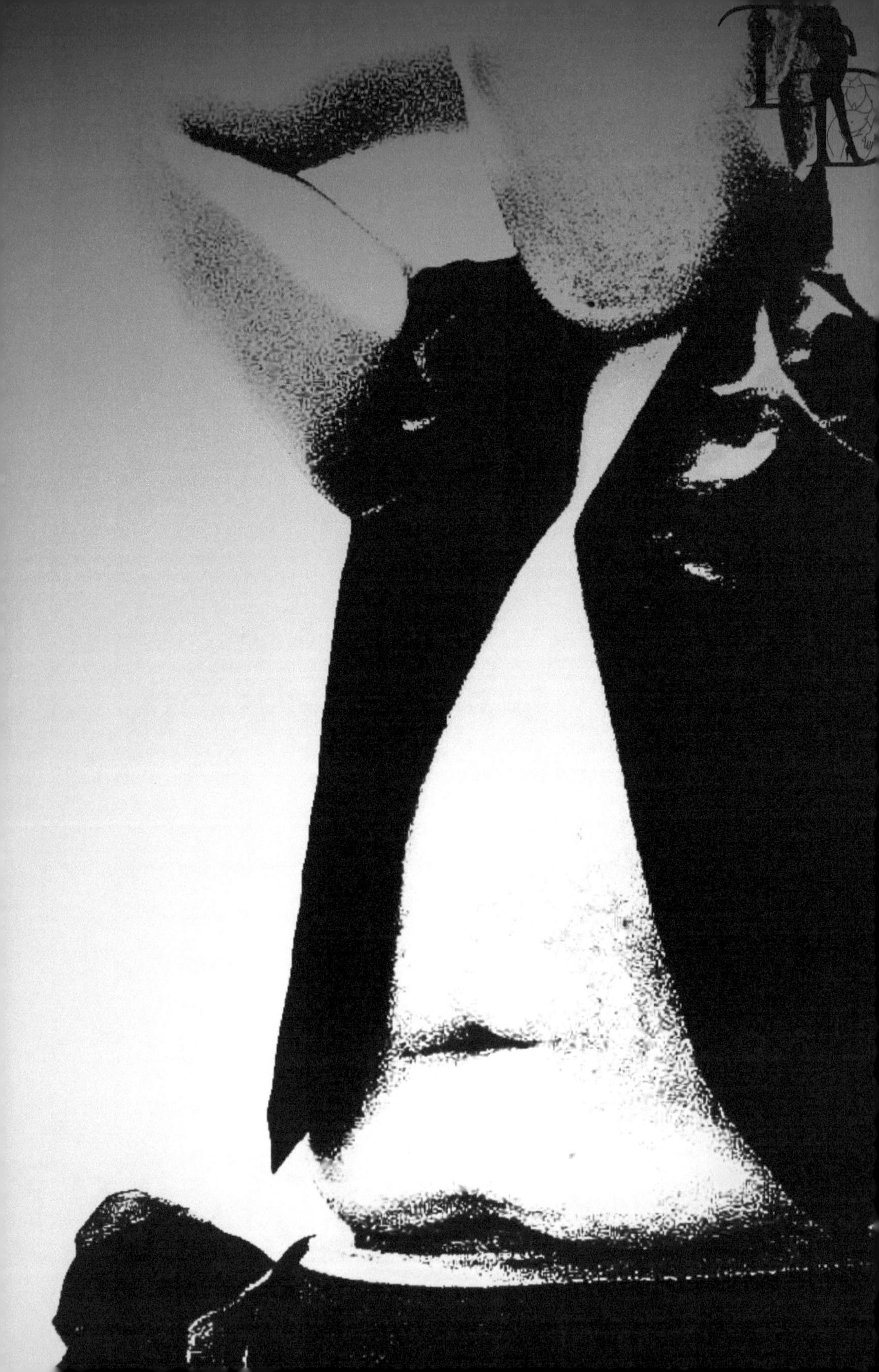

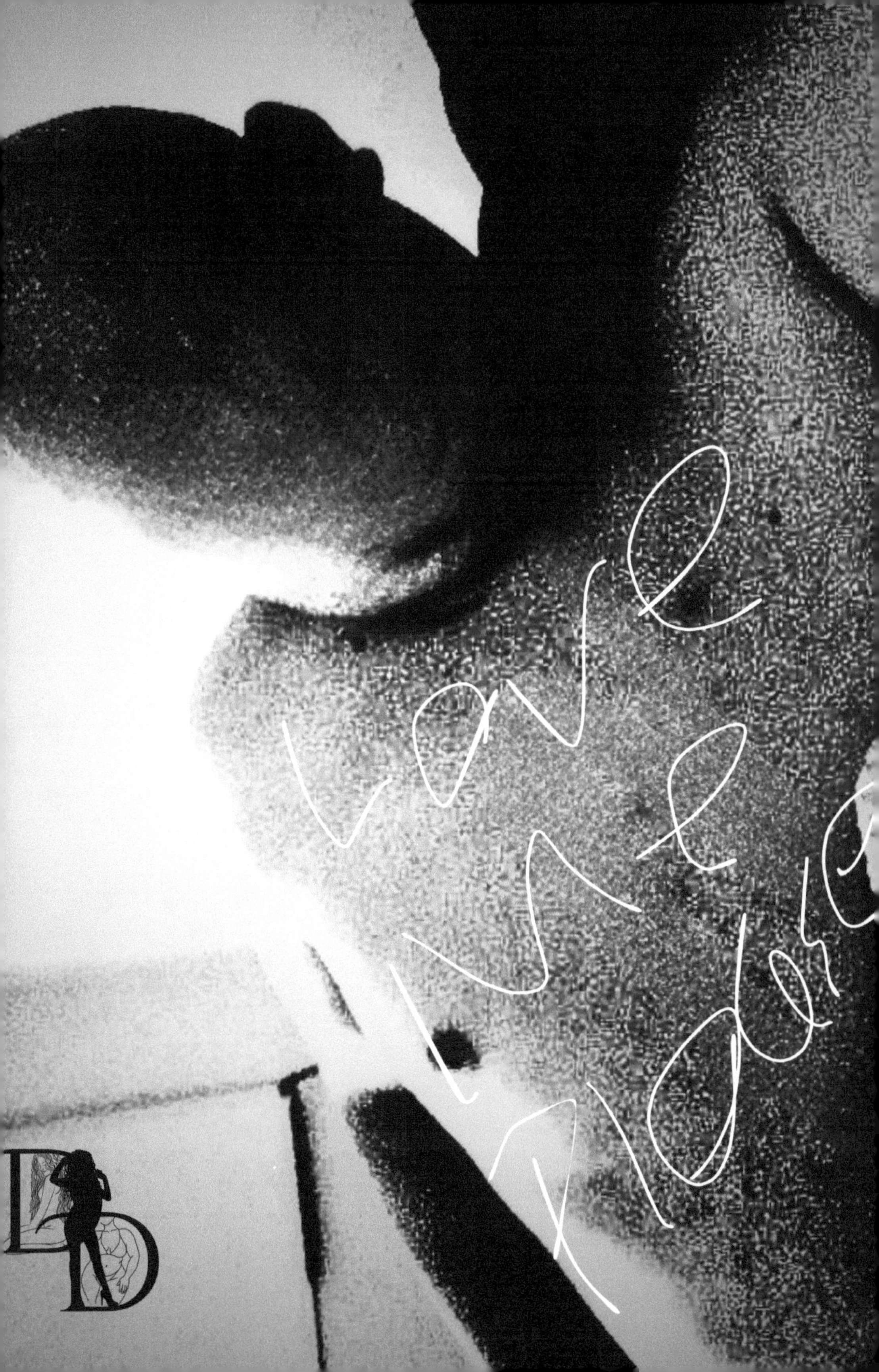
Love
me
harder

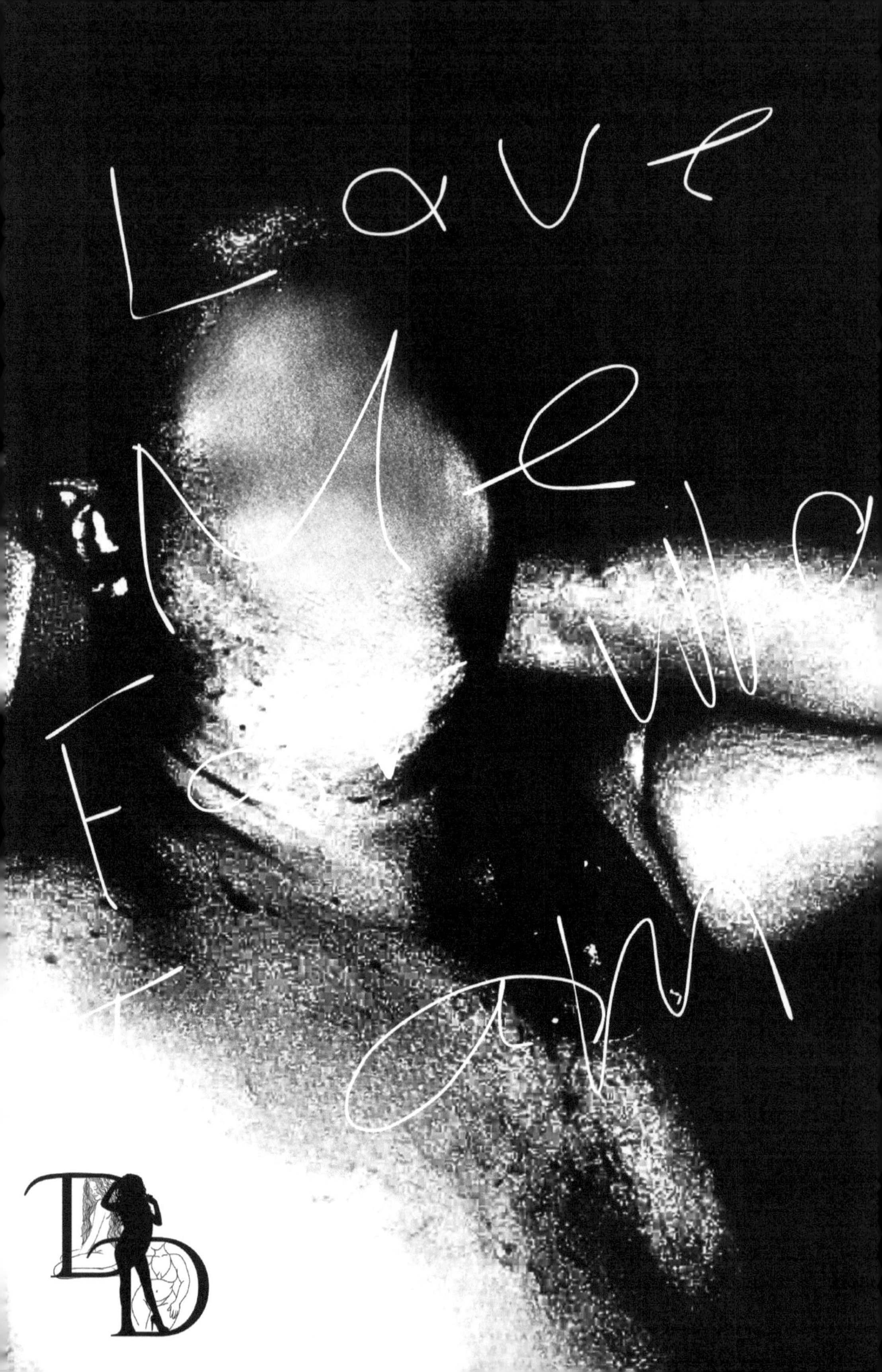
Love
Me
who
For
own

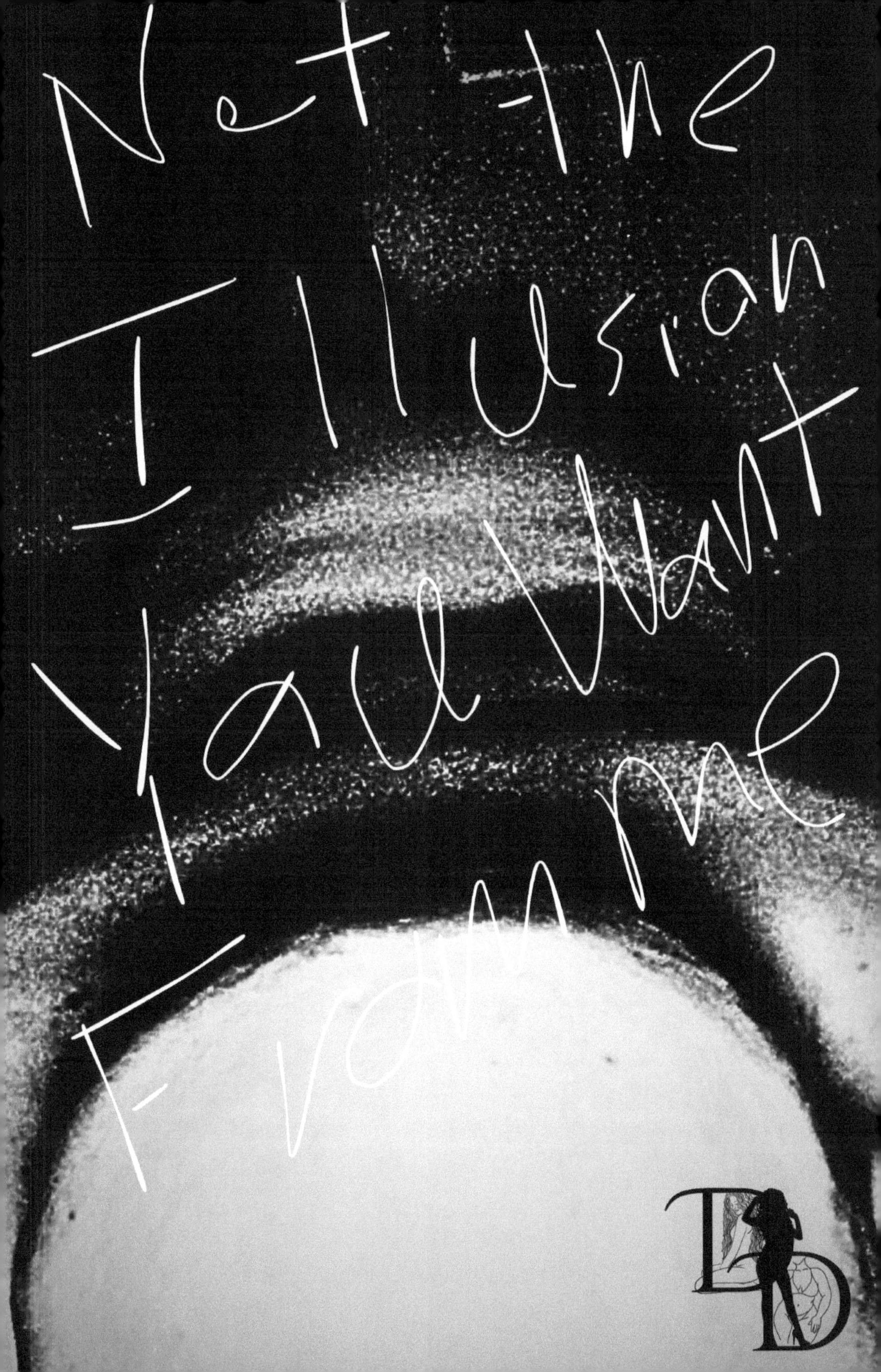

Not the Illusion
You Want
From me

But will you see me

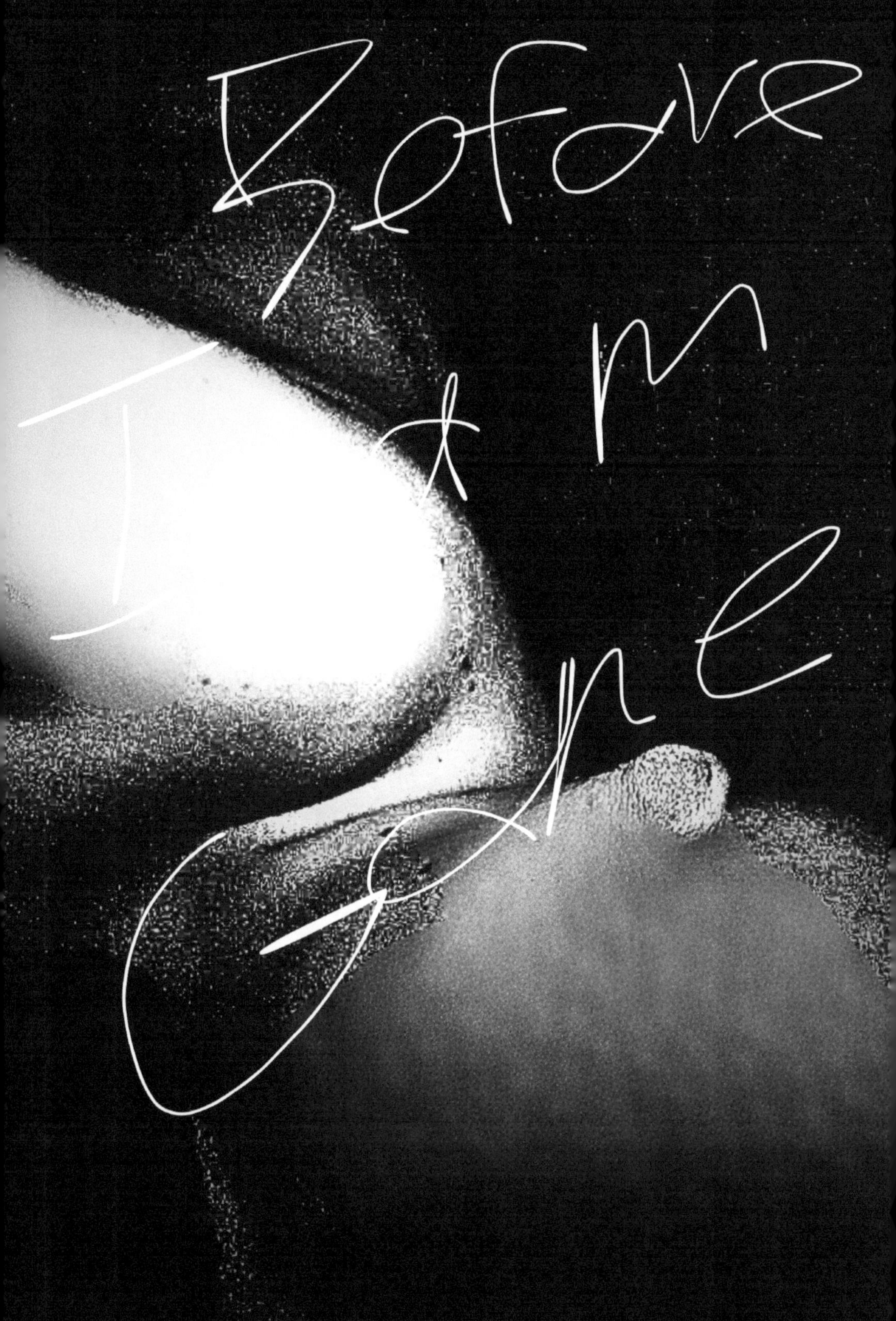

Before
I'm
Gone

www.ingramcontent.com/pod-product-compliance
Lightning Source LLC
Chambersburg PA
CBHW040930110726
48006CB00001B/136